D0542652

BUILDINGS
OF BRITAIN

Lavenham

BUILDINGS OF BRITAIN

ROGER FITZGERALD

BLOOMSBURY

Acknowledgements

I would like to thank everyone at Bloomsbury, particularly Kathy Rooney, and also Kate Bouverie, Jenny Parrott, and the book designer, Neysa Moss. Amongst the many things I owe to my parents is my first interest in buildings and architecture. Roland Wearing developed my enthusiasm for art at the Perse School, Cambridge. At the School of Architecture, Manchester University, it was Derek Dearden's and Ron Brunskill's teaching which probably had the greatest effect on the shape and style of this book. My partners at Architects Design Partnership have encouraged me in this particular form of 'continuing professional development' (as the current jargon would describe it); but the greatest sacrifice has been my wife's, who has travelled the length and breadth of the country, visiting obscure regions with me, and been available for comment at all hours on the latest text or illustration.

ILLUSTRATIONS:
FRONTISPIECE: Church at Cullompton
PAGE VII: Stamford
PAGE XI: top: Lewes, bottom: Rye
PAGE XII: agricultural worker's house
and barn

First published in 1995 by Bloomsbury Publishing Plc, 2 Soho Square, London W1V 6HB

Copyright text and illustrations © 1995 by Roger FitzGerald

The moral right of the author has been asserted

British Library Cataloguing in Publication Data

A CIP record for this book is available from the British Library

ISBN 0 7475 2148 4

10 9 8 7 6 5 4 3 2 1

Designed by Neysa Moss

Printed in Italy by Graphicom

To Lynne, James and William

Contents

Introduction

THIS IS A VERY PERSONAL book. It does not set out to be comprehensive, or even scholarly. It contains illustrations of places and buildings selected to make particular points; the aim is not to educate, but simply to encourage the reader to look closely at places he or she knows or comes across. Most of the places described I visited over a twelve-month period, and this book is therefore not unlike a sketchbook or diary, complete with the spontaneity and vividness that this might imply.

It has been fun to write, and I hope it will convey something of the great pleasure which can be derived from exploring the immensely varied buildings in Britain.

Many books on architecture are structured in a straightforward manner, either analysing buildings through history, or geographically. Others describe the different stylistic approaches. I have taken a different angle, and instead approached the subject at a number of levels. Firstly, buildings are considered in terms of their broad context, in both the physical and the historical sense. Then they are discussed individually in relation to their different uses. Finally, the decoration, detail and materials – the smaller parts that make up whole structures – are described.

Rather than glamorizing places, I have presented them as they really are. Many guidebooks are beautifully photographed in flattering or quite extraordinary lighting conditions, and inevitably a visit is then a disappointment, with the presence of other tourists, cars and indifferent weather failing to meet our high expectations. Because one can be selective, and may add emphasis to certain elements, drawings and paintings can often make specific points better than photographs. To produce a painting you have to spend a few hours with your subject; you get to know and understand it. Understanding is the key. We do not comprehend our environment or our heritage enough; and this is why, when we make our contribution to it, all too often we make mistakes.

PAINTING, SOME PERSONAL NOTES

I started painting about ten years ago. Sitting on some rocks at Abermawr in Pembrokeshire, I tried to paint the cliffs, the sky and the sea – and I must have had a dozen or so failed attempts. I still have some of them and they are dreadful. I knew this at the time and almost gave up before I had started.

I cannot recall how I came to discover John Blockley's books which teach watercolour techniques, but without them I would not have persevered. Gradually I learned some methods and copied some illustrations. It is quite difficult for many architects to paint, as our normal drawing work tends to be methodical and precise. Paintings need to be looser, to

allow the viewer's eye to do some work, and to leave parts of the image open to interpretation.

Working to a publisher's deadlines, one can become tense, as the last thing you want is to have to throw a painting away. This can be a vicious circle, as tension often leads to work which is too precise and sterile. Many times I had to tell myself, 'I don't care if this painting gets chosen or not, slap on the paint!' My art teacher used to say 'paint from the elbow', which proved to be good advice.

Also influential has been the work of John Knapp Fisher, who has a tiny studio at Croesgoch, Pembrokeshire, where he paints and sells his work. His paintings are inspirational, with large expanses of dark textured areas contrasting dramatically with small light patches left to indicate a cottage or a boat.

Although most pictures were done in a single hectic year, this book covers a period of about five years. Inevitably the styles vary, and I make no apology for having experimented along the way.

Usually I start by setting out the size of the painting within which I draw in the main shapes and proportions. After this I do the line drawing with a fine pen. Setting the picture up like this is almost always rather tedious, but then the fun starts. Usually I paint in the windows and heavy shadows using a brush and black ink. This suddenly brings the painting to life. Colour washes are then added. Quite often I will leave it all to dry completely at this point. Later, looking at it afresh is exciting as well as useful. There is still time to add more washes if necessary, and then to highlight plants, people, cars and particular features.

I tend to use only two or three favourite brushes and just half a dozen or so colours: burnt and raw sienna, indigo, burnt umber, yellow ochre, cyanine blue, aureolin and cadmium red. I use drawing ink for black, and masking fluid to create any white areas.

There are all sorts of tricks to learn, what with rubbing candle wax, flicking toothbrushes and dipping sponges. However, these techniques can easily become an end in themselves.

I try to draw and paint as quickly as I can; this gives vitality to the work. Also, it is far better to stop the painting too early than to overwork it. Of course we all find our own ways of doing things – this is part of the fun, developing a personal style.

BUILDINGS
IN CONTEXT

I NDIVIDUAL BUILDINGS THEMSELVES provide a fascinating field of study, but so often it is not just a single structure that we look at but a group of buildings. The first question to ask is why they are there: what were the forces that brought them about, and why in that particular place? It may have been a strategic military stronghold, or a remote religious enclave, or it may have been to take advantage of a natural feature such as a harbour or ford.

Often the impact made by a group of buildings is greater than one would expect if each one is studied on its own. The spaces between them can be as important as their actual form, and especially so where there is a formal arrangement. Planned external spaces are comparatively rare, and planned towns and villages still more unusual. Piecemeal and haphazard development is far more common, which creates an informal and thus a very different relationship.

Although buildings are static objects set in space, we, the observers, move through those spaces and get ever-changing views. This, after all, is how we experience our towns, by moving through them. The way buildings relate to each other and to their surroundings is just as important as how a building may be viewed on its own.

ILLUSTRATION PREVIOUS PAGE: Richmond Castle

GREENWICH AND CANARY WHARF

In all of London, the finest relationship between buildings, landscape and the River Thames can be found at Greenwich. Central to the composition is the Queen's House, designed by Inigo Jones between 1616 and 1635. This is framed on either side by the domes of the Royal Naval Hospital. Colonnades and formal lawns are interspersed between the buildings and sweep down to the riverside walk. Venturing inland, the landscape becomes less formal, and rises steeply to Greenwich Park and Blackheath. It is the best place for young children on a summer's afternoon in South-east London.

The view North from the top of the hill has changed greatly in the past decade. The old classical composition remains ordered, restrained and dignified; towering beyond are the new Docklands developments of Canary Wharf, a clutter of competing, speculative buildings that sadly do not relate to the formal Greenwich axis.

Prehistoric

We do not fully understand the origins of Britain's prehistoric monuments, and this gives them a mysterious, even frightening quality. Sometimes huge lumps of stone have been shaped, such as at Stonehenge, while elsewhere, like at Avebury, the slabs have been left unworked.

The monuments are best seen with the sun at a low angle, or even in moonlight, lighting conditions which accentuate the rough texture of the stone surface and which cast long, dramatic shadows.

STONEHENGE

Stonehenge was built of pillars of bluestone, created by natural frost action which shattered huge lumps of stone from its parent hillside, Foel Drygarn in the Prescelly Hills, in Pembrokeshire. Astonishingly, it seems that they were hauled on sledges down to the sea where they were floated on rafts around to and then up the Bristol Channel, before being pulled to their site in Wiltshire.

Exactly the way this was done, and how Stonehenge was built, and why, has been the matter of much speculation. The fascination of Stonehenge lies in the questions it raises, its dramatic appearance (particularly in changing light), and its enduring ability to attract visitors.

PENTRE IFAN

Close to the source of the Stonehenge stones in the Prescelly Hills, and overlooking Cardigan Bay, Pentre Ifan occupies a majestic site. Its capstone is enormous, weighing about sixteen tons, balanced precariously on three vertical stones. A fourth upright forms a portal at the South end, where several smaller stones define a crescent in front of the chamber. Much of the delight in visiting it is derived from the isolation of its location and, unlike at Stonehenge, one can walk among the stones.

CARREG SAMSON

Neolithic man held the dead in great reverence and built great chambered tombs. Carreg Samson is about 5000 years old, and sits high above the sea at Abercastle. Three upright pillars support a massive horizontal capstone; the space between these pillars would have been infilled with drystone walling to form the enclosed burial chamber, or cromlech. The whole structure would than have been covered by earth and stones, which has subsequently been eroded by the elements.

Defence

Compared with on the Continent, there are relatively few settlements in Britain which needed defensive walls. But some were built, however, and parts have survived, although much was demolished in the 18th and 19th centuries to make way for development.

The present-day street patterns often suggest where the defences used to be, with much tighter-packed buildings within them. (For example, in Wisbech there are early 19th-century crescents, built around the castle mound and following the lines of the original defensive wall.) Military history has thereby had a direct influence on contemporary street layouts.

The best surviving walls can be seen at York and Chester. York's walls are not as complete, and are more noteworthy for the fine gates they contain, providing access to the city (see page 51).

Because military strongholds were inevitably the regional powerbase, they became inseparably linked with local, and even national government.

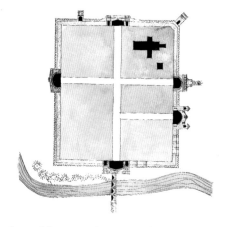

CHESTER

In Chester some of the original Roman masonry has survived, principally in the North and East walls. The walls on the other two sides of the city were later rebuilt. It is still possible to walk on the walls, and to complete a circular route of about two miles with excellent views into the city and out to the Cheshire countryside.

In the middle ages, Chester's wall had several towers, particularly on the East side of the city. The best known of these is King Charles's tower, from which Charles I saw his army defeated in 1645.

The gates to the city were grand structures, and the whole complex must have formed a powerful and dramatic structure rising out of the landscape.

EDINBURGH

Edinburgh has been built on seven hills. At the heart of the city is an extinct volcano, Arthur's Seat, which was probably the location of an Iron Age fort. Edinburgh Castle sits on top of this, a proud and robust building which appears to rise seamlessly out of the rock. Indeed its original name was Duneadain, meaning 'fort on a slope'

and it is likely that this has been an important defensible location for considerably more than a millennium.

Edinburgh became Scotland's capital in 1437, and until the union of 1707, was where the Scottish Parliament met, in Parliament House.

With its military and political importance, it was inevitable that the city would also become Scotland's leading centre of culture and learning, with many theatres, concert halls, galleries and museums, and its famous annual arts festival. It has remained an unspoilt Georgian city, comparable with Bath (see page 37) for its refined and dignified architecture, in a romantic and idyllic landscape.

Cathedrals

Cathedrals are more than just individually fine buildings; they have had a major influence on the settlements which developed around them.

In most cathedrals, construction work on them has been virtually continuous, providing a steady flow of work for building tradesmen. In particular, the cathedrals which were monastic in origin generated considerable quantities of produce from their farmed estates, encouraging local markets.

Besides offering employment and trade because of their size, cathedrals have also been major generators of local wealth, learning and culture.

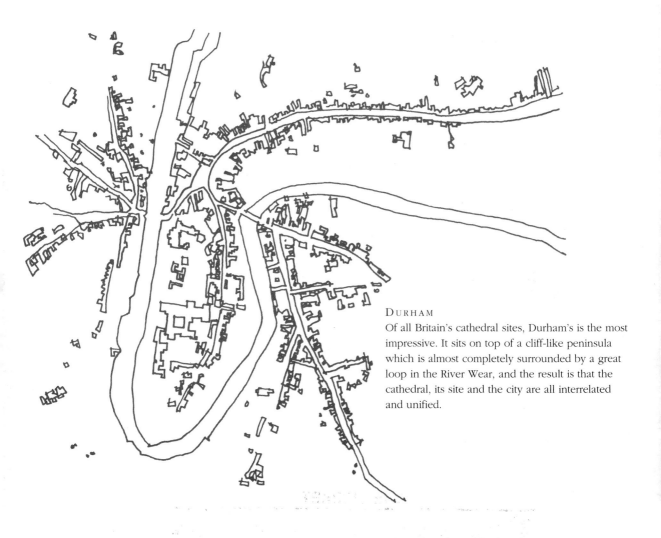

DURHAM
Of all Britain's cathedral sites, Durham's is the most impressive. It sits on top of a cliff-like peninsula which is almost completely surrounded by a great loop in the River Wear, and the result is that the cathedral, its site and the city are all interrelated and unified.

LINCOLN

Seen high above the rooftops, Lincoln Cathedral is an expression of the early English and decorated Gothic styles. The whole building is beautifully proportioned, and its central tower and two West front towers dominate the city.

There is a tremendous sense of verticality, and obviously the setting helps with this impression, being high on a hill. The corner turrets to the towers, the pinnacles, the steeply-pitched roofs – every device has been used to give a vertical emphasis, and the building seems to reach up to the heavens.

Ports

Fishing ports are full of character and charm; just the presence of the sea uplifts them, bringing drama in heavy seas, and calm reflections at other times. Often rugged quay walls rise sheer out of the water. The buildings need to be tough and solid to withstand the conditions but, in contrast, are often brightly coloured.

LOWER FISHGUARD

Lower Fishguard was once quite a large port with a busy fishing trade. The buildings are stretched out, following the quayside. Heading inland is the Gwaun Valley, formed by glacial overflow and not by the small stream which runs along it now. The valley, harbour and the houses are all unspoilt and, although the fishing industry has declined, there are plenty of leisure boats filling the harbour.

STAITHES

Staithes is made up of huddles of fishermen's cottages, built of robust materials. Everything is functional and there are no concessions to unnecessary decoration or attempts at the picturesque; it is a very practical working village.

The natural harbour is sheltered on either side by huge headlands, but the sea is chasing Staithes inland through erosion. Three times it has stolen the Cod and Lobster Inn.

WHITBY

The granite walls of Whitby harbour rise out of the sea to give a solid rugged base to the town's buildings. Houses stack up on the hillside, and on the East cliff they are topped by the 12th-15th century abbey, its ruins silhouetted against the sky.

The quayside is busy, with fish stalls and fish restaurants, amusement arcades and rows of gleaming white seats looking out to sea.

CLOVELLY

Clovelly is quaint. The main street is cobbled, steep and narrow, and tiny courts and alleyways lead off on either side. The descent from the clifftops to the 14th-century harbour is 400 feet and far too steep for cars, which have to be left at the top. There is a large car park with a modern visitors' centre built in 1988, and this has the effect of keeping most of the cheap knick-knacks in one place and away from the main street.

Brightly coloured buildings tumble down the hillside, with enticing glimpses of the harbour below. At one point the street opens out with two long vistas to the sea on either side of a cottage which somehow clings to the cliffside.

POLPERRO

Polperro's origins are in the fishing industry, although this has now declined and tourism is more important to the local economy. Its attractive harbour is lined with pleasant, though quite plain Georgian houses. There are some unattractive modern buildings, and indeed the individual buildings of all ages are not distinguished, but the whole group is greater than the sum of the parts. The village is enclosed by steep cliffs, on which small whitewashed houses have been built.

Markets

Markets were held at least once a week. Stalls were erected for the day, and rent paid to the overlord. Some markets were specialized, such as the wool market at Chipping Campden.

Many towns had a formal market square, while others had a less-planned space, such as the triangular sloping site used in Ashbourne, Derbyshire. The clarity of this space has been lost by the later addition of buildings within the triangle; the market continues to be held, but in a less attractive space than the original. In other towns, like Moreton-in-Marsh, the main street was widened to accommodate the market.

RICHMOND

Richmond marketplace is one of Britain's most dramatic outside spaces, surrounded by buildings. It has even been likened to the famous piazza in Siena, Italy. This view is from the Norman castle (started in 1071) which still dominates the town from its marvellous site. The outer edge of the market is a spectacular horseshoe-shaped sweep of fine 18th-century buildings, on radiating burgage plots (see page 16). The buildings follow the line of the old town walls, built as defence against the Scots in the 14th century. Cutting through this ring of buildings are narrow alleyways, known locally as 'wynds'.

In the Middle Ages, Richmond's markets (fish, other foods, and knitted stockings) were very important and served a large area, and this open space provided an ideal setting. The markets brought considerable wealth to the town,

BEVERLEY

Beverley is a really lovely small town, full of attractive buildings, and with pedestrianized streets which enable you to stand back and enjoy them. From the quality of decorative detail on the buildings, it is apparent that Beverley was once a particularly prosperous town. This was on account of its wool trade and flourishing marketplace. At the centre of this space is the market cross, of 1714, an ornate structure whose decoration includes the arms of Queen Anne.

indicated by the fine Georgian buildings surrounding the square. The shop fronts which have been added later are mostly a rather undistinguished collection of alterations, bearing little relationship to the detail and scale of the upper levels.

At the centre of the marketplace is an irregular assortment of buildings including the Chapel of the Holy Trinity, and the obelisk (1771). Far from detracting from the space, these monument-type buildings act as focal points. It was raining when we visited, but several people were still using the obelisk steps as a seat and meeting place.

It might be argued that the marketplace is not improved by all the cars and buses that park there and block the square. I disagree: they bring colour and activity to a space with could otherwise seem dead and drab.

Growth of Towns

Under the feudal system villagers were granted strips of land, cottages in which to live and some grazing rights. In return they had to work on the lord of the manor's farm at certain times.

However, some villagers such as the carpenter or the blacksmith were not directly involved with agriculture. They were exempt from the feudal system and instead had a different tenancy, the burgage plot. They had to pay a fixed annual rent to the manor for the land, and the tenancies could be bought and sold.

The burgage plots were long but narrow, which minimized the valuable street frontage taken by each plot. Frequently a regular rhythm can still be seen along old street frontages, created by the consistent width of the plots (as in King's Parade, Cambridge, below). Typically, there would be a shop on the ground floor with living accommodation above. The rear of the site, often reached via an alleyway from the front, would be used for kitchens, stores, stables, workshops or a vegetable garden. Later, adjoining plots were amalgamated in some towns where land was scarce, such as Tewkesbury. In Chipping Campden, where there is less demand for land, the rear of the sites have usually been left undeveloped.

CAMBRIDGE: KING'S PARADE
The East side of King's Parade demonstrates that even with different heights and styles of buildings, the burgage plots give the street a regular rhythm of plots of equal width. Half-timbered medieval houses sit alongside rebuilt formal Georgian facades – the result has variety, but within a controlling framework.

TOTNES

Totnes became a busy port in the 16th and 17th centuries. An assortment of different buildings line the High Street, all of similar width as they were built on burgage plots. This regular rhythm and the use of a limited range of materials and colour give the street a degree of unity, which is nicely balanced by changes of direction, the irregular rooflines and the variety of detail.

Note the shopfronts, which seem to belong very naturally to the buildings over them; so many town centres have shops utterly divorced from what happens above.

Mining

Mining, and coal mining in particular, dominates the surrounding landscapes and social structure completely. Now many mines are closed, leaving environments full of irony: places which created great wealth and opportunity, so little of which was shared by the communities which toiled so hard; the great awe-inspiring machinery now standing derelict and worthless.

LEVANT BEAM ENGINE
Cornwall has an abundance of derelict engine houses and stacks which once served its tin and copper mining industry. Some engines were used to pump water out of the excavations, while others were used to raise men or ore to the surface.

The Levant Beam Engine is the oldest in Cornwall, dating from 1840. It has not worked since 1930, but has been refurbished by the National Trust. Its location is dramatic, perched on a cliff close to Land's End.

WELSH MINING VALLEYS

The Rhondda is the best known of the Welsh mining valleys. At the Lewis Merthyr Colliery site there is now a visitors' centre, with exhibitions recording the history of the area.

Brightly coloured terraces line up on the hillside, one behind another, originally squeezing still more workers into an area already grossly overpopulated. The terraces generally follow the contours, but occasionally one lurches diagonally across at a peculiar angle. Every so often the terraces stop and there is a different building, such as a school or a chapel.

Transport & Waterways

The relationship between architecture and transport has always been close. Before the last century one thinks of groups of cottages huddling around a harbour, or on either side of a bridge at an important crossing point of a river. Canals became an important means of transport and attracted a particular type of building. More recently came the great railway stations and airports, huge termini handling the arrival and departure of vast numbers of people.

SKIPTON

Waterside buildings have a special quality. One only has to visit Venice to appreciate this; the palaces are fine constructions in their own right, but it is the canals which give them their magical quality. The same applies, although to a much lesser degree, in Skipton.

The Leeds and Liverpool Canal passes through the town. The canal is 127 miles long and rises to 500 feet above sea level as it crosses the Pennines, linking these two important industrial cities.

Some of the mills and warehouses, once built to serve the canal, have now been converted to museums, restaurants and for other leisure uses, while others are derelict. Houses line the sides of the canal and are reflected in the water. There are bridges, locks and towpaths, and the bright red machinery used for unloading the coal barges provides a cheerful contrast with the local grey stone (see opposite). Pleasure barges pass up and down, bringing in tourists. It is all very charming, not least because there has been no attempt to create something picturesque. Everything is simple, practical and functional, and one never quite forgets that this was built as a working environment; it would all be very ordinary without the canal.

BRADFORD-ON-AVON

Bradford-on-Avon gained great wealth from the weaving industry and all routes from the surrounding area converged upon this crossing point. The town's prosperity enabled the building of fine stone houses, terraced up from the river.

The stone bridge was largely rebuilt in the 17th century, although two of the original arches survive. The building on the bridge is a chapel, subsequently also used as a lock-up.

LIVERPOOL

Liverpool was once a very small harbour; quays were added in the 18th and 19th centuries. Trade developed, particularly with North America, and by the reign of Queen Victoria, Liverpool had replaced Bristol as Britain's major transatlantic port. Canals were built to link Liverpool with Manchester, Birmingham, and their surrounding satellite towns.

The finest dock is Albert Dock, built 1841-5. It has survived both wars and subsequent redevelopment, and now its original character has been sensitively preserved. Huge iron doric columns on the ground floor create an arcade, and support the brick elevations above. The detailing is on a grand scale and very robust.

On the day I visited Liverpool the Tall Ships Armada was returning home, and every vantage point on the waterfront was taken. The huge crowds and splendid buildings made an impressive spectacle. Liverpool has been fortunate in having avoided the rather crass development which has spoilt other docks, such as Hull and London.

HULL

Hull is a very old port. Docks were constructed on either side of the wide Humber estuary, and it became a deep sea fishing port and a trade outlet for Yorkshire and the East Midlands. The docks were bombed and badly damaged during the Second World War.

One of the docks has been filled in and a shopping centre built on it. Another dock, closer to the sea, has been made into a marina. The docks have become very touristy, retaining little of the old, tough character. Alongside, between the old town and the sea, a modern housing estate has been built which could be anywhere; it does not exploit the proximity of the sea, nor does it turn away from the dual carriageway. There is no response to the unique character of Hull, nor to the problems and opportunities of its specific location.

If you want to see something of the old Hull, go and look at the original quayside where the old town backs on to the river. There is great diversity and visual interest, but it is all very dilapidated. No doubt there will be pressure to develop the frontage in the future. The challenge will be to preserve the essence of the existing character.

Planned Towns

All towns have been planned. Some thought has gone into all major decisions, such as the best place to cross the river or the most prominent location to position the church or castle.

Certain places have received extra, far-sighted planning, however, which has been able to control development over the centuries; such towns have a special sense of place.

There are also those settlements which have been designed in their entirety, such as new industrial centres, whilst others provide a new way of life for people leaving the cities.

LUDLOW

Between 1086-1094 the castle was built at Ludlow, to secure the border with the Welsh. A new town developed alongside to provide the garrison with services. In the early 12th century the town walls were built, and within them a rectilinear street pattern was established complete with burgage plots (see page 16).

Ludlow's importance increased both in relation to its strategic control of the Border country and Wales, and to its wool and cloth trades. The town buildings are dignified and imposing, and the layout of the streets is appropriately formal. The parish church has a 135-feet tower which together with the castle dominates the town's skyline.

BURY ST EDMUNDS

Even before the Norman Conquest, Bury St Edmunds was an important town, with a small Benedictine monastery. In 1081 Abbot Baldwin began an ambitious plan to rebuild and enlarge the town, based on a regular grid of streets. Within this, two rectangular spaces were set aside for markets: one, Angel Hill, opposite the 14th-century gateway into the abbey, survives as a car park; the other, Buttermarket, has been partially built on.

When Churchgate Street was set out it was aligned on an axis with the great West door of the abbey, with the wonderful mid-12th-century belltower on the same axis.

The abbey was lost in the Dissolution but Bury St Edmunds remained a wealthy market town. The formal street pattern was kept, and provided the perfect layout for later Georgian development. The individual buildings are attractive although fairly plain, but the rectangular street grid ties everything together, unifying the different types of building.

EDENSOR

In 1839 the 6th Duke of Devonshire decided that he did not like the view of Edensor from his home, Chatsworth House, and so he moved it.

Joseph Paxton, who designed Crystal Palace, produced the layout for the new village. Every house is different, with an extraordinary variety of styles: classical, Gothic, Jacobean, Norman and Swiss. The collection is unified by the use of a single material, a mellow gritstone.

The houses are set at angles, with generous expanses of lawn sweeping down to the road.

LETCHWORTH GARDEN CITY

Living in an industrial town in the late 19th century was not pleasant; housing was squalid, sanitation bad and pollution severe. Ebenezer Howard hoped to change this, and in 1898 published a book, *Tomorrow: A Peaceful Path to Real Reform*, which discussed how to combine industry with the environmental advantages of country living.

In 1903 two architects, Barry Parker and Raymond Unwin, started work on plans for a prototype for Howard's ideas, Letchworth. Industry was located on the East side of town so that prevailing winds would blow fumes away from residential areas; housing was concentrated close to the places of work.

SALTAIRE

In 1850 Sir Titus Salt, having made his fortune, started building Saltaire, near Bradford. This was a new town on a greenfield site with good canal and rail links, designed to provide better conditions for his 4000 mill workers. Seven storeys high and over 500 feet long, the mill dominates the town, its chimney visible from everywhere. Built on the banks of the Leeds and Liverpool Canal, it is in a grand Italian Renaissance style.

The rest of the town is a series of parallel streets of nearly 800 houses, well-built in sandstone with a variety of decorative detail (see window on page 124), in the same Italian Renaissance style. Salt provided other facilities to complete the town: welfare accommodation, a school, public baths, a large park and allotments, and an attractive classical church. In all, Saltaire was a most advanced example of town planning.

Buildings & Landscape

Sometimes buildings sit like monuments surrounded by landscape but completely divorced from it. Elsewhere the two are inseparable, greenery submerging the buildings which themselves extend out into the landscape.

There is, of course, a place for both approaches. What is beyond doubt is that the two must be considered together in order to provide a coherent whole. All too often the landscape is an afterthought, or not even thought about at all.

OXFORD HIGH STREET

Once established, streets tend to maintain their original alignment. Oxford High Street, known locally as the High, has acquired its delightful gentle curve simply because the old track from Carfax, the junction of four streets and centre of the Saxon settlement, to the bridge across the River Cherwell (on the site of the present Magdalen Bridge), followed the same route.

This curve gives the street much of its interest, constantly changing one's views up and down.

The outside of the curve faces South and therefore the sun, and has finer buildings than the other side.

It also has the Tree, which is one of the most important plants in the country. It is a mature sycamore located between Queen's and All Soul's Colleges, and is the one significant natural form in a street of formal, man-made objects. It is the ideal contrast to the surrounding buildings, and by good fortune it has the maximum impact; its positioning is perfect, right in the middle of the outside curve.

CHAGFORD

Some places owe their beauty to their setting. Chagford is such a place, sitting at the foot of the surrounding hills, sheltered and enclosed. The individual buildings are attractive but ordinary; what is special is the relationship with the enveloping landscape.

ELY CATHEDRAL

Before the fens were reclaimed, and Ely itself was developed, the distant views of the cathedral rising out of the water must have been remarkable. Even today it stands above, and completely dominates, the flat fenland countryside.

Most of the cathedral was built between 1081 and 1189 in the Romanesque style. At the crossing of the nave and transepts there was once a Norman tower. This collapsed in 1322 and was replaced by an octagon, an exceedingly elegant and imaginative structure, which allows light to flood down into the heart of the cathedral.

RYE

Originally Rye was virtually surrounded by the sea. Set up on a sandstone hillside, it was an important port. The harbour silted up 400 years ago and the sea is now some distance away.

Lining the narrow and cobbled streets, Rye's houses showcase a variety of materials: brick, tile-hanging and stained weatherboarding. These variations and the steeply-sloping streets give a most picturesque appearance, and the town is popular with tourists.

BURFORD

Shortly after 1323 a bridge was built across the River Windrush at Burford. It became an important bridging point, and the town grew by serving the local sheep farmers. Eventually trade reduced, and in 1812 the London to Cheltenham road was re-routed South of Burford. The town was bypassed and declined, thereby escaping radical rebuilding.

Today most visitors approach the town by turning off the A40, and descend the impressive wide High Street leading down to the old bridge. The width of the street is a mixed blessing, with cars parked on either side and two-way traffic. Over 100 cars filled the view I painted on the summer Saturday we visited the town.

The buildings have been preserved in fine condition, the shopfronts entirely in keeping with the domestic scale and traditional materials of the street. Most of the roofs are superb stone specimens laid in diminishing courses. Compare some of the other roofs, like the slate on the post office, to see how much better stone blends with the stone walls.

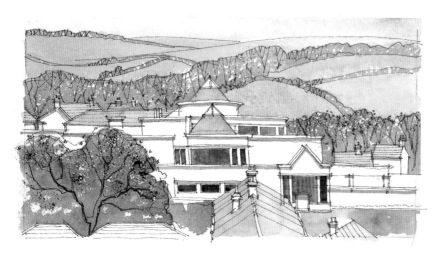

TRURO

The new Courts of Justice building at Truro is a major modern public building, sitting on high ground and visible from many other parts of the town. The conical rotundas, covered with local slate, are above waiting areas and provide an impressive focal point for the composition. Less dominant is the pedimented portico, which clearly indicates the entrance. This is crisp and simple modern design which fits in well with its surrounding landscape.

SHAFTESBURY

Passing down a tiny passageway which leads off Shaftesbury High Street, a remarkable sight comes into view. First, on the left, you see stone cottages plunging down the hillside, which is so steep that there is virtually a storey-height difference in level between neighbouring houses. Then, over the rooftops you have a magnificent panorama of the Vale of Blackmoor, idyllic rolling Dorset country-side. On the right are the rugged buttressed walls of what was a Benedictine abbey until the Dissolution. The street itself is paved with cobbles and setts. There is a lovely contrast between the textures and enclosure of the street and the vast openness of the hills and sky beyond.

BUXTON

Virtually every town and city in the country has at least some ribbon development, and nothing better demonstrates the need for planning controls.

Buxton provides a particularly nasty example: driving North out of the town on the A6, and on the edge of the Peak District national park, a long finger of unattractive houses reaches out, cutting across the spectacular landscape.

TISSINGTON

Approaching the village from the Ashbourne to Buxton road one passes along a half-mile avenue of lime trees which gives the village a sense of privacy; it seems as though at any moment you will reach a private country house.

The village is an informal arrangement of stone houses on either side of a wide open space, with lawns on either side of the road running through the village. One of these houses is the Elizabethan Manor House, occupied by the FitzHerbert family. Opposite is the church, set on high ground and half hidden by sycamores and yews.

A stream runs through the village and at the South end is a large duck pond. The surrounding countryside is unspoilt, making Tissington and its setting one of the most special places in Britain.

ST GOVAN'S CHAPEL

This 13th-century chapel looks as though it has been carved out of the landscape. Built of stone, it sits across a narrow slot between two cliff faces.

The approach is dramatic; leaving the car park, the grass suddenly stops and the cliffs plunge straight down to the sea. Steep stone steps lead down to the chapel. The floor is of earth and the building blends completely with its setting.

ST DAVID'S CATHEDRAL

Most cathedrals were built on high ground and dominate the landscape, as epitomized by Lincoln, Ely and Durham. St David's is different; nestling in a hollow, only its tower can be seen from any distance. Thirty-nine steps lead down to the cathedral from the plateau on which the tiny city, no larger than a village, has been built.

The local purple sandstone was used; rather dull in colour and with the austerity of the detailing, it is in keeping with the rugged yet beautiful scenery of this part of Pembrokeshire. In spring, clumps of daffodils, bright yellow, delicate and transient, contrast with the solid permanence of the cathedral.

Inside the decoration is considerably richer than outside. The most memorable feature is the floor, which slopes steeply up from the West door to the high altar.

Open Spaces

It is worth drawing a distinction between two very different types of external space found in towns and cities: streets which are narrow, dynamic spaces suggesting movement, and squares which are static open areas capable of accommodating activities of various kinds. Great civic spaces were primarily market squares but are now often used as car parks. Private residential squares, whose central gardens provide an attractive formal setting for grand houses, have more often retained their original use.

Streets developed gradually. Sites were sold as building plots with tenants free to erect what they wanted. Once established it is very expensive and disruptive to alter the street layout. The result is the unpredictable layout which adds so much to the character of our town centres and there is the additional benefit that it slows down vehicles.

It was not until the 17th century that whole streets were conceived of as a unified element such as in Bath (see page 37).

EXETER: CATHEDRAL CLOSE
In the close at Exeter on the East side of the cathedral, charming medieval houses for the clergy look over its lawns, where it is lovely to sit. The value of spaces like this is inestimable. What is remarkable is their simplicity: the paving is very straightforward; there are trees, and places to sit, and grass. There is no unnecessary fuss. For something to look at there is of course the cathedral, which has two fine Norman towers and some highly ornate stone carving on the West front.

SALISBURY: CATHEDRAL CLOSE

Several of Britain's cathedrals are surrounded by informal precincts or closes incorporating buildings associated with the cathedral, such as the Bishop's Palace, clergy houses, and so on. As relations between the clergy and local townspeople were often not good, the closes were surrounded by high walls and entered through gates.

This was the case at Salisbury, where the gates are still closed at night. This helps create a feeling of separation, with the close having a unique and special character, the finest cathedral setting in the country. It is surrounded by a fascinating assortment of buildings in various styles, built between the 14th and 18th centuries. The Bishop's Palace is a huge building, occupied by the cathedral school. The buildings on the North and East sides create the character of a street, while those to the South and West are more imposing individual villas. Mompesson House, in Choristers' Green, is owned by the National Trust and is open to the public.

Of course, the close is dominated by the cathedral itself (see page 47), with its tower and spire the highest and most exciting in the country. There have been relatively few changes to the cathedral, making it the purest surviving 13th-century example in Britain. The sweeping lawns around it have not always been so open; James Wyatt carried out improvements between 1789-92 which included demolishing a huge belfry and rationalizing the landscape.

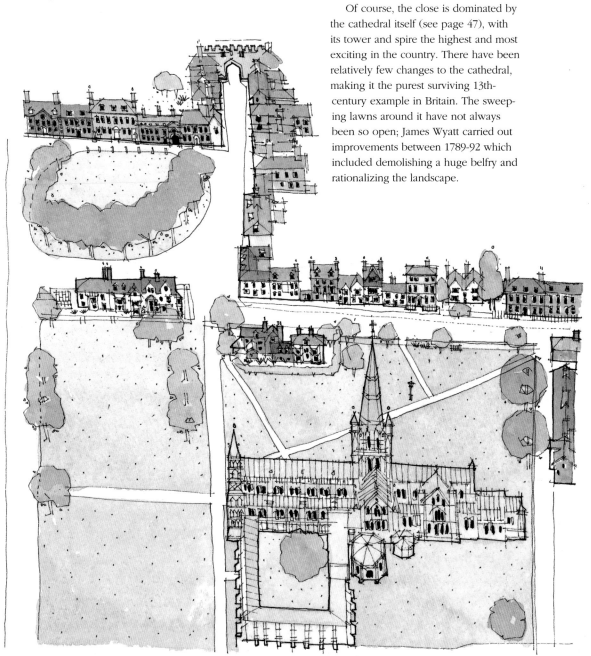

LONDON: DORSET SQUARE

The location was originally fields beyond the
Marylebone Road, which were then developed by
Thomas Lord. It was also where the first great
cricket matches were played, becoming the home
of the Marylebone Cricket Club (the MCC), and
Lord's Cricket Ground was here until the lease
expired in 1810.

In the 1790s the first houses in the square
were built, on the nearest side to the centre of the
capital, the East.

There is uniformity and consistency in all the
elevations facing the square, because the building
blocks are treated as a whole. The individual
houses still have the original fanlights above the
front door, and generally there is stucco on the
ground floor, decorative ironwork, and amazingly
slender glazing bars subdividing the sash windows.

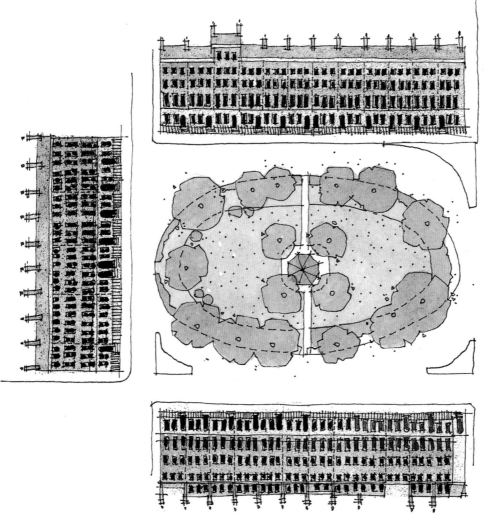
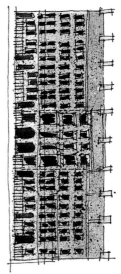

BATH: ROYAL CIRCUS AND CRESCENT

Bath is an exceedingly elegant city, matched in Britain only by Edinburgh. John Wood the Elder began the huge programme of urban rebuilding in 1729, with Queen Square. Leading off this is Gay Street which comprises a series of similar terraced houses which step up the steep hillside. The local stone has been used; where it has been cleaned recently it has a glorious honey colour, most beautiful in the late evening sunlight.

At the top of Gay Street lies the Circus. Begun in 1754, the year of John Wood the Elder's death, it was completed by his son in 1769. This is one of my favourite places in Britain: the scale and proportion of the buildings and the circular space

at their centre are just right.

The masterstroke is the layout of roads into the Circus; wherever you enter there is always a sweep of curving buildings opposite, closing off your view. This emphasizes the views you do get down the street on either side as you move into the space. The facades of the houses have been beautifully crafted and detailed.

There are five huge plane trees at the centre of the space, planted by the Victorians, and they are magnificent specimens, although probably a little big, blocking views and light. However, they are a good foil to the buildings, providing contrasting colour and texture.

TEWKESBURY: ALLEYS

Tewkesbury has an informal, constricted centre. It is surrounded by the flood plains of the Rivers Avon and Severn as they converge, so areas of dry land became valuable and congested. Narrow burgage plots had frontages onto the main streets. In the 17th century the rear areas of these sites were developed, with long narrow alleys at right angles to the main streets providing access and daylight. With the land shortage, buildings of three or even four storeys were erected. Up to 90 alleys were created, of which only about one third remain.

Tewkesbury Abbey was a Benedictine monastery and it was the last to be dissolved by Henry VIII. It has survived as a parish church, the townspeople having bought it for £453 from the king. Many views of its beautiful tower can be glimpsed from the town's streets.

YORK: LOWER PETERGATE AND THE SHAMBLES

York has some of Britain's best surviving medieval streets or, as they are known locally, 'gates' (derived from a Scandinavian word meaning street). The quaintness of their appearance is matched by their names: Lower Petergate, The Shambles, 'snickleways' (alleys), 'Whip-ma-whop-ma-gate' and Goodramgate (which boasts Britain's oldest terrace, of 1316).

The Shambles, built between 1350 and 1450, was the 'Fleshammels' – the street for butchers, wide shelves in front of the shops, and hooks above for displaying meat. The upper floors were canti-levered out, so much so that neighbours could open their windows and shake hands with each other. The street is almost covered overhead giving the scene below a sense of intimacy and enclosure.

 THE SURREY INSTITUTE OF ART & DESIGN

STOW-ON-THE WOLD

Stow-on-the-Wold has a wide high street, ideal for an open-air market which creates a grand, spacious place for shopping and plenty of space for parking vehicles. The perception of the buildings is completely different to a view from a narrow street, where the street sides are seen obliquely (for example, see York, page 39). At Stow-on-the-Wold it is possible to step back and view buildings – like this inn – from the front, seeing the whole elevation at once.

NOTABLE
BUILDINGS

E ARLIER I EXAMINED some of the spaces created between buildings, and described a selection of the best settings for them. Now I will consider their details and decoration, and more importantly, the buildings themselves.

Buildings exist to meet our needs. Historically these would have included worship, defence, trade, or simply somewhere to sleep. Today our needs are different, and include leisure, more complex retailing and better housing. In the past there have been periods of much innovation in the areas of education, health, transport and prison building.

This diversity is echoed by variety of form, scale, style and decoration, as can be seen by contrasting the great Victorian rail stations and museums with a simple dovecote or a beach hut.

Virtually every building meets a different functional brief, and the way in which it adheres to this is a measure of its success. This section aims simply to indicate the immense range of requirements and solutions.

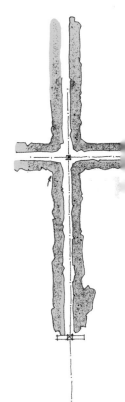

ILLUSTRATION PREVIOUS PAGE: York: Monk Bar

CASTLE HOWARD

Castle Howard is a fine example of how architecture and landscape can be integrated, each complimenting the other. The long approach to the house is a carefully controlled sequence of events: the road from York undulates following the lie of the land and passes through two gates, the outer marking the edge of the estate. Between an avenue of trees, there are glimpses of the house and its gardens.

Eventually the road reaches an obelisk, 100 feet high and built in 1714. This marks a change in axis of 90 degrees, from the avenue to the drive, which leads directly to the North side of the house. Here the architect, Sir John Vanbrugh, broke with tradition; the house, rather than being orientated East/West, as normal, instead faces North/South, thereby maximizing the views available. The house is in a grand baroque style, with a flamboyant dome over the Great Hall.

The landscape incorporates countless architectural features: the stables, the temple of the Four Winds and Hawksmoor's Mausoleum. There are statues, pyramids and water features everywhere, and lakes to the North and South. The formal gardens include the rose garden and Atlas fountain. It would be difficult to define where the buildings stop and the gardens begin, so closely are they integrated.

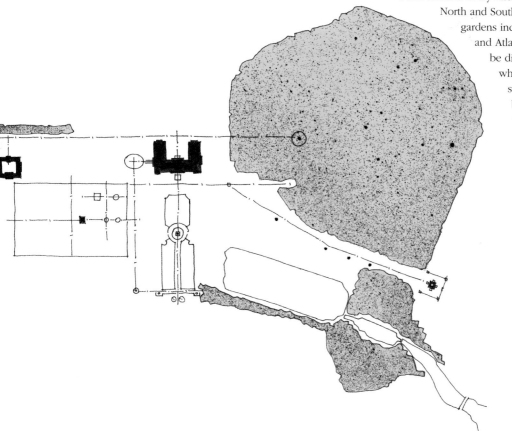

Religious Ruins

The ruins of religious buildings have a unique, melancholy atmosphere. They are unlike other disused buildings in that they still seem to have some purpose. A ten-pin bowling alley that is no longer wanted has virtually no use; it is redundant. By contrast, a derelict religious building still retains an atmosphere of awe and majesty. Indeed, in some respects it is its abandonment and neglect which enhance these attributes.

COVENTRY CATHEDRAL

Coventry Cathedral, a very different ruin to Rievaulx, is the result of German firebombs in 1940. Sir Basil Spence won an architectural competition after the war to design a new cathedral, and he brilliantly combined this with the remains of the 14th-century structure.

Both the new building and the ruins are full of symbolism; the most memorable is a cross made by two burnt oak beams lashed together and set at the East end of the old cathedral. Behind this simple cross, carved in stone, are the haunting words 'Father Forgive'.

RIEVAULX

I was immediately enchanted by Rievaulx. The tourists had gone home, and the valley of the River Rye was silent. Around the abbey are a few rose-covered cottages; one was producing a lovely aroma from the wood burning in its hearth. Rising above everything were the grand and dignified ruins of the abbey, at one with the serene setting.

Cistercian monks tended to choose remote spots for their abbeys. (The Benedictines and Augustines preferred to have their monasteries in towns and cities, places they then influenced considerably.) The Cistercians sought solitude,

although their choice of location was restricted by needing a good supply of water.

Founded in 1131 by a few monks who were sent there by St Bernard of Clairvaux, 'Rievaulx' comes from the French translation of Rye Valley. A market town, Helmsley, grew up at a respectable distance from the abbey (see page 49).

Rievaulx was suppressed in 1538 by Henry VIII, and was soon looted for building materials, lead and timber, thus exposing the walls to the elements. Built in the local fine-textured sandstone the walls survive still, one of Britain's loveliest ruins.

Cathedrals & Churches

Britain's greatest building achievement is perhaps represented by its thousands of medieval churches and cathedrals. The Gothic style suited the religious spirit of the Middle Ages, with soaring towers, spires and pinnacles reaching towards heaven, solid West fronts and heavy porches symbolizing gateways into the House of God; and ornate carvings in wood and stone, and pictures in stained glass giving artistic expression of religious stories.

LAVENHAM

Many of our finest parish churches were built with the proceeds of the wool and cloth industries, and there was great competition between adjoining villages to have the finest church. Usually the churches were built of stone. An exception to this is in East Anglia, where flint was used along with stone to create exceptionally well-built churches.

The church at Lavenham is one of the finest examples. The town is the centre of a wool and cloth trade which generated the vast wealth needed to build on this scale. With its tower at 141 feet high, and exquisite flush flintwork walls, the church presides over the town, perched on a hill at the top of the High Street.

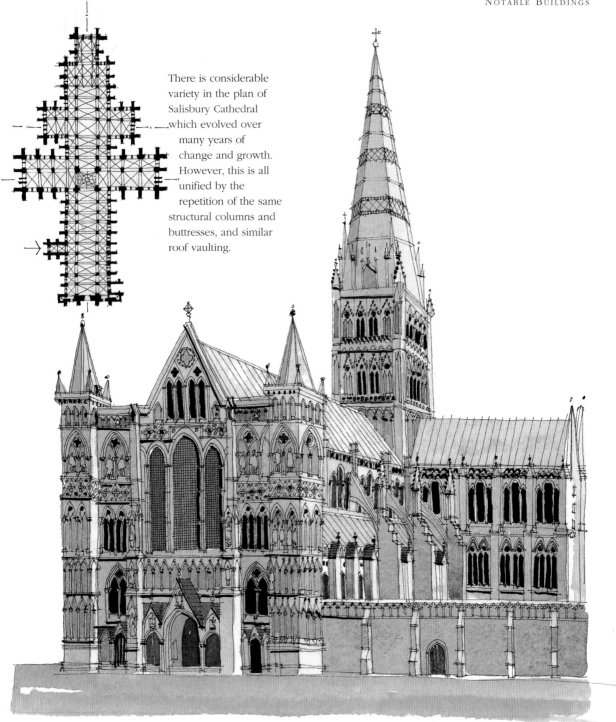

There is considerable variety in the plan of Salisbury Cathedral which evolved over many years of change and growth. However, this is all unified by the repetition of the same structural columns and buttresses, and similar roof vaulting.

SALISBURY CATHEDRAL

The cathedral at Salisbury is probably the most representative of all the English Gothic cathedrals. A central tower at the crossing of the nave and the transepts is a typical characteristic, and at Salisbury this structure continues upwards with a spire, the highest in the country at 404 feet. There are secondary transepts, a large cloister (to the South of the nave), a North porch, a square East end, and a polygonal chapter house.

Comparison with French cathedrals is intriguing: these are higher with apsidal East ends and double aisles; they have their towers at the West end. Transepts and cloisters are often absent and the setting is frequently more 'urban'.

BEVERLEY MINSTER

There were previous churches on this site, and the present buildings were begun in 1220. Beverley Minster is a rarity among parish churches in that it has three towers (the only others are at Selby in Yorkshire and Melbourne in Derbyshire).

Built in magnesian limestone it is a large and magnificent building, a staggering undertaking considering that it is effectively just a parish church.

The best view is from Beverley Westward, from where one can see the splendid Gothic West front. Most visitors will first see the view illustrated, as they approach from the town centre along Highgate; it really does look just like a medieval cathedral city.

HELMSLEY

Originally just a tiny settlement, the stature of Helmsley increased when a Norman castle was built there. However, its history is more closely entwined with a religious building: once Rievaulx Abbey was built nearby, Helmsley served as its market town. It became quite important and managed to retain trade even after the dissolution of the monasteries. Today, its prosperity remains linked to Rievaulx, providing restaurants, pubs and shops for visitors to the nearby religious ruins. The dominant building in Helmsley is All Saints' Church, built by the Victorians.

HORSMONDEN

Salisbury, Beverley and Lavenham all represent spectacular undertakings. Smaller parish churches are usually relatively more modest buildings, but socially and visually they still provide the major focus to a village.

Horsmonden Church in Kent is a good example, even though it is positioned away from the centre of the village, and the church interior is actually quite plain. Its beauty arises from the relationship between the elegant and embattled church tower with the nearby barns and oasthouses from which the tower emerges, and the meadows, hop-fields and trees of the local landscape.

The West tower is ordinarily the dominant external element of the British parish church; internally it is often a fine timber roof. The planning of a typical church is simple: the entrance is through a doorway in the West tower or through a projecting South porch; the nave has aisles, while the chancel does not.

Military

The earliest military defences simply utilised features in the landscape, such as a hill or a sharp bend in a river. Simple man-made barriers were added. The development of military architecture came with the Normans. Immediately after their conquest they built hundreds of castles and town walls all over the country. In both cases the weakest element was the gateway, and so evolved the fortified gatehouse to defend it.

With the Crusades came opportunities to study Byzantine military buildings, and consequently British castles and fortifications became more ornate.

Military buildings were welcomed by royalty as they symbolised and ensured local stability and ultimately the authority of the sovereign.

As time went by the rather utilitarian keep and fortifications of the military castle were replaced by more comfortable manor houses. These still retained defensive features at first, but the by the 15th century the type of building had effectively evolved into a purely domestic form (see Residential, page 94).

BEVERLEY: NORTH BAR
As the capital of the East Riding of Yorkshire and with an important market, Beverley needed to defend its status with town defences, which were interrupted with four, or possibly five, gates or 'bars'. North Bar, built in 1410, is the only survivor.

The gates were both functional and also expressions of civic pride. North Bar is an early example of the use of brick for such a building.

On either side of the gateway, inside the walls, are classical townhouses. The gatehouse closes off the view, the road narrowing to a single lane to pass under the arch. This is attractive, except that nowadays traffic inevitably builds up; vehicles, controlled by traffic lights, can only pass through in one direction at a time. In a way, this tightness and congestion ensures that North Bar remains a gateway.

YORK: BOOTHAM BAR

York still has roughly two miles of medieval walls. The section between Monk Bar and Bootham Bar is particularly interesting, with views across well-kept gardens towards York Minster.

Monk Bar and Bootham Bar are not just practical defensive buildings with portcullises and slit windows, but are also designed to inspire awe.

Castles

The first great castles were built in Britain during the 11th and 12th centuries by the invading Normans, and should be seen as the physical expression of the feudal system of government which they imposed upon the native Anglo-Saxons. Robustly built to withstand attack, the main role of the Norman castle was as a centre of local government and justice.

The subsequent fate of these castles has varied greatly: some have fallen into ruin, while others even today house courtrooms or jails. Many are now occupied by wealthy families, while others have passed into the ownership of organizations such as the National Trust or English Heritage.

CRATHES CASTLE

This outstanding 16th century tower house is a short distance inland from Aberdeen. It is an example of a style of building which developed as a transition was made from the rugged fortress, built to be defended (such as Edinburgh Castle), to the comfortable country mansion (such as Balmoral).

The massive granite walls and the tower-form of Crathes are castle-like and defensive, while the conical roofs, turrets and projecting top floor are flamboyant and picturesque.

The wing on the right-hand side of the tower house is Queen Anne in style, but had to be rebuilt in 1966 following a fire. The impressive yew hedges were planted in 1702.

POWIS CASTLE

There has been a castle here, just outside Welshpool, since Norman times. The present buildings were originated by the Gwenwynwyn family during the reign of Edward I; in return for the site they had to renounce any claims they had to Welsh princedom.

In 1587 the castle was bought by Sir Edward Herbert, who began the process of converting a military stronghold into the Elizabethan mansion which remains today.

The castle sits high on an outcrop of rock, with the gardens stepping down in four large terraces below. These were laid out by William Winde in the 17th century, and remain largely unchanged since then.

LEEDS CASTLE

Leeds Castle owes its beauty largely to the spectacular setting; 500 acres of parkland surround the castle, which itself is positioned in the middle of an artificial lake, made in the 14th century for defensive purposes, with a connecting bridge to the mainland.

The walls of the castle rise sheer from the water, giving stunning reflections. The castle buildings, built in the local wealden sandstone, are best seen on early summer evenings when they glow honey-coloured in the low sunlight.

A wooden castle was originally built here in the 9th century, and was replaced by a stone one during the 12th century. It was a defensive fortress until it was made into a royal palace by Henry VIII.

BALMORAL

Queen Victoria's husband, Prince Albert, bought this lovely estate in 1852. A curve in the River Dee, and the surrounding forested hillsides, still provide a tranquil place for the royal family to take their holidays.

The original castle was rebuilt by Prince Albert in a romantic Scottish baronial style, with projecting turrets and conical roofs contributing to a lively and picturesque skyline.

CAERNARFON CASTLE

A castle surrounded by water, such as this one, creates a very different image to one standing high on a craggy outcrop, like both Stirling and Edinburgh castles. The result, however, is similar, and the Welsh must have been overawed when in 1286 Edward I ordered this castle to be built, a powerful symbol of his rule over Wales.

Built on a commanding site on the Menai Straits, thirteen massive towers and huge walls dwarf the surroundings, and drawbridges, portcullises and gigantic ramparts add to the awesome effect. A small town, occupied by the English, was built alongside the castle, protected by walls; the local Welsh people had to make do with settling outside the town walls.

These spectacular medieval defences provided the setting for the investiture of the Prince of Wales in 1969. Nowadays the sheltered Menai Straits are busy with pleasure craft, while the castle teems with tourists.

Public Buildings

Municipal corporations expanded considerably in the second half of the 19th century. To meet their spatial, functional and symbolic requirements, huge and spectacular town halls were built.

The most impressive of these were in the North. Great Gothic monuments were erected to express wealth and civic pride. Bradford, Bolton, Halifax, Leeds, Manchester ... all vied with each other to have the most magnificent town hall. Liverpool was slightly different, opting for a classical style, but just as ornate and impressive nonetheless.

ABINGDON TOWN HALL
Built between 1678-82, this building follows the traditional pattern of a public meeting room on the first floor, over an open arcaded ground level (see Guildhalls, pages 60-1).

It is a very attractive building, with big Corinthian pilasters and pleasing proportions, all of which helped Abingdon to become the county town of Berkshire (although it later lost this status to Reading). The only unsatisfactory part is the rear, which has a strange, asymmetrical and lumpy stair tower.

The town hall was designed by Christopher Kempster, a Burford mason who worked with Wren, and who obviously acquired from him a keen eye for scale and proportion.

MANCHESTER TOWN HALL ➤

In 1866 an Act of Parliament was passed to create space in the centre of Manchester for a new town hall and square. A competition was held, and won by Sir Alfred Waterhouse. The site for the town hall was an awkward triangular shape, but Waterhouse's design exploited the geometry brilliantly. Smaller accommodation follows the perimeter, and the centre is occupied by the Great Hall and lightwells.

Built in a 13th century Gothic style, the main features of the interior are the magnificent corridors and staircases, whilst externally the dominant element is a 286 foot clock tower.

◄ ABINGDON PRISON

This is a building which has had a number of different uses: it was built between 1805-11, to the designs of J. Wyatville and D. Harris, as the county jail; in 1868 this was closed and it became a corn warehouse; it is now used as a leisure centre.

The jail was built just after a period when thousands of prisoners died from typhus during the late 18th century. This led to a wave of prisons made to new designs, with better ventilation. For the first time prisoners were put into separate cells, supposedly to encourage them to reflect on their past misdemeanours.

Transport

There has always been a close relationship between places and the means of travelling between them. Mass transportation systems did not come about until the 19th century, and when they arrived with the railways, the style and scale of the architecture were suitably decorative and monumental.

The finest were the great railway termini, and even today one marvels at their scale and grandeur. Modern buildings like Stansted Airport, and the Channel rail terminus at Waterloo, show that we can still emulate the achievements of a century ago.

The most popular means of transport today is the private motor car. The buildings associated with this form of transport are not distinguished. Motorway service stations are devoid of any local character, and petrol stations are frequently crass features on the edges of towns and villages.

PADDINGTON RAILWAY STATION

This enormous train shed was designed in 1850 by Isambard Kingdom Brunel with Matthew Digby Wyatt. The basic layout of the design was straightforward, with three arched 'tunnels' facing West, receiving and discharging trains. Adding interest and complexity are two transepts which cut across the main roof areas. The detailing of the various connections was clearly given plenty of thought, although one wonders how many passing passengers even give them so much as a second glance.

Early this century a fourth roof was added. It was designed to match the earlier bays, although it would probably have been better if something contrasting had been produced instead.

SOUTH MIMMS SERVICE STATION

There is an extraordinary contradiction about the motorway service stations we build today. We travel to them in our sophisticated cars, capable of cruising at well over 100 miles an hour, complete with air conditioning, CD players, heated wing mirrors and mobile telephones. More than anything else we own, our vehicles represent up-to-date technology. We pull into the motorway service station, and there it is, dressed up as a pseudo-vernacular group of old farm buildings. The car park is a sea of tarmac, and there is no covered route from areas of parking to the entrance of the buildings.

I am not sure who is responsible for the design of these places, but if the motorway service station was chosen to represent the age in which we live, what a confused, unimaginative and inappropriate image that would be!

Market Halls

In some towns, trade became the dominant factor. Market halls were built to provide shelter for the traders, commonly an open, arcaded ground floor, with enclosed meeting rooms on the level above.

In the 12th and 13th centuries, merchant guilds were established; they were associations of merchants and generally they met in guildhalls.

Huge covered markets were built in the 19th century, when shopping arcades became popular. In this century, these evolved into the shopping mall; more recently, out-of-town retailing, with convenient parking, has become the vogue.

THAXTED GUILDHALL

Thaxted Guildhall was built around 1390 by the Cutlers Guild, at a time when the town was a centre of the knife and blade industry. It became the town hall when the industry declined, and later a grammar school. The building was restored rather insensitively in 1910, and more tastefully in 1975.

The ground floor is open with a stone flag floor, and this would have been the main trading area. The first floor was for meetings and the top floor provided accommodation for the guild warden.

The top two floors overhang, giving the building added emphasis. It sits at the top of the village street, with attractive timber-framed buildings on either side.

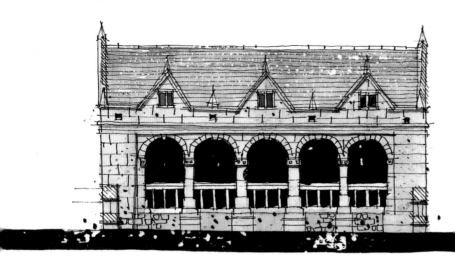

CHIPPING CAMPDEN

In Chipping Campden, as at Ledbury, space was formed for the market hall by widening the street. However, here the similarity ends, for the Chipping Campden building is very different in character. Built in 1627, it is a single-storey arcade, constructed in stone.

LEDBURY

In Ledbury the High Street widens at one end to create a triangular space for the town's market. This is dominated by the early-17th-century market hall.

The building is a free-standing structure, with an open ground floor with stone flags. Sixteen 16-inch by 16-inch oak pillars sit on stone plinths and carry the upper level. This is of timber, with square panels (so characteristic of the West Midlands), and diagonal bracing. It is possible to trace the structural logic of the building in a few moments, and worth contrasting with some modern timber-framed structures where the timber is often applied just for decorative effect.

Many of the streets in Ledbury, such as Church Lane, are narrow, cobbled and intimate, and this adds to the impact of the market hall when these spaces open out into the square, providing a convenient and pleasant place to shop..

Shops & Arcades

The nature of shopping has changed radically over the past century or so, and it has become a major tourist and leisure activity. Groups of shops have been brought together to form covered and pedestrianized arcades, making dry, pleasant and safe shopping environments, and there are huge department stores which sell virtually everything.

The real problems today are created by the out-of-town stores, which are drawing the trade and activity from the historic high streets. They also create environmental and traffic problems on the edges of our towns.

CHESTER: THE ROWS

At Chester there is a most unusual arrangement of shopping on two levels, known as 'the Rows'. Various theories have been advanced to explain how this has come about. The most likely explanation arises from a fire in 1278. Stone undercrofts were then built to provide greater protection to the timber-framed buildings above. Originally these undercrofts were used for storage, but subsequently were found to make very good shop units. Above, at first floor level, there is a public walkway which is arcaded to carry the overhanging buildings above. The shops are set back from the frontage.

The arrangement maximizes the use of the floor area, and the first floor galleries make one feel like pausing to overlook the streets below; it is more of a promenade than a pavement, and makes shopping a pleasant experience.

HARRODS

In the Brompton Road of
London's Knightsbridge, filling a
whole block, is Harrods. Built
between 1901-5, it is lavish and
enormous. I am not sure
whether I prefer it at night,
when thousands of white lights
outline its shape and main features, or during the day, when all
of the extravagant terracotta
work can be seen. The most
impressive part of the interior is
the art nouveau meat hall.

TUNBRIDGE WELLS: THE PANTILES

Tunbridge Wells only developed in the 17th century, after the discovery of its springs. Very accessible from London, and with attractive surrounding woods, it became very fashionable.

The Pantiles, a colonnaded walk, was first laid out in 1638 and now forms a unique pedestrian precinct. On a gentle curve, with an agreeable mixture of white weatherboard and red brick and tile, it is a most civilized shopping environment.

Worryingly, Tunbridge Wells has recently acquired a large and successful commercial development at the other end of the town centre, and one can foresee retailers in the Pantiles being tempted to move closer to the new shopping area.

BURLINGTON ARCADE ➤

The first arcade to be built in London was the Royal Opera Arcade, built between 1816-18. The advantages of a pleasant, sheltered and clean environment for shopping, away from the filthy, uncovered streets were quickly recognized.

The Burlington Arcade is the longest of London's arcades, and what could have been a rather boring tunnel, is relieved by changes in height and width. The arcade has undergone many changes due to fire, fashion and bombs. Even so, it remains a well-preserved example of a 19th-century shopping arcade.

◄ BARTON ARCADE, MANCHESTER

The origin of the shopping arcade lies in Paris in the late 18th century. The idea was imported into this country, and became very popular in the 19th century. The Victorian arcades are infinitely better than today's, which lack the same confidence, exuberance and richness of detail.

Barton Arcade, built in 1871, links Deansgate to St Anne's Square in Manchester. There is no doubt that to be successful, arcades need to be on busy through-routes, or shortcuts.

The glass and ironwork have clearly been influenced by the great railway stations, and give the arcade a fine quality of natural light.

Industry

Industrial buildings are fascinating to study, as there is such a close relationship between the process housed within the building and the form that was built to accommodate this function.

With such a vast range of different manufacturing processes and with the invention of new techniques, there is great diversity in industrial architecture. A lesson that was learned early on was the need for flexibility to allow for change in the future.

TOTNES: WAREHOUSES

Taking advantage of its important location at the head of the Dart Estuary Totnes became an important trading centre, (see page 17).

Lining the River Dart, on either side, are warehouses with brick and stone facades and slate roofs. They seem to rise straight out of the water. Once an area bustling with work and activity, today the river is frequented by pleasure boats.

MANCHESTER: WAREHOUSES

Manchester provided the market-place for the produce of the mills on the lower slopes of the Pennines, to the North and East of the city. Warehouses were needed close to the railway stations and canals, not just for storage but also for displaying goods to potential buyers. The warehouse was therefore an important symbol of the company which occupied it, and consequently they were grand and ornate buildings, influenced by Italian palaces and the Gothic style.

This railway warehouse is in Lower Byron Street. Built in 1880, it accommodates a railway siding along its length, is three storeys high and 300 feet long. It is now a museum.

CROMFORD: COTTON MILL

Cromford was developed by Sir Richard Arkwright as an industrial community (see page 69). In 1776, he built North Street for his weavers. The ground and first floors provided conventional living accommodation. The distinctive feature is the second floor, which housed handlooms to make fabrics from the yarn produced at the mill. These top-floor workrooms were lit by large windows.

CROMFORD

Sir Richard Arkwright was a brilliant inventor, producing ideas and machinery so far ahead in its thinking that he was accused of witchcraft in his native county, Lancashire.

He moved to Cromford, a remote spot in the glorious Derbyshire countryside with strong water power and lower costs. Arkwright developed the small village into a busy town. He built sturdy houses for his workers (see page 68), and a church, school and inn. His first factory, producing cotton from a spinning wheel driven by flowing water, was built in 1771. Two years later Arkwright built another, Masson Mill at Matlock Bath.

Soon there were other imitators, first in Yorkshire and Lancashire, where cotton mills were driven by the fast-flowing streams, and later abroad in the USA and Germany.

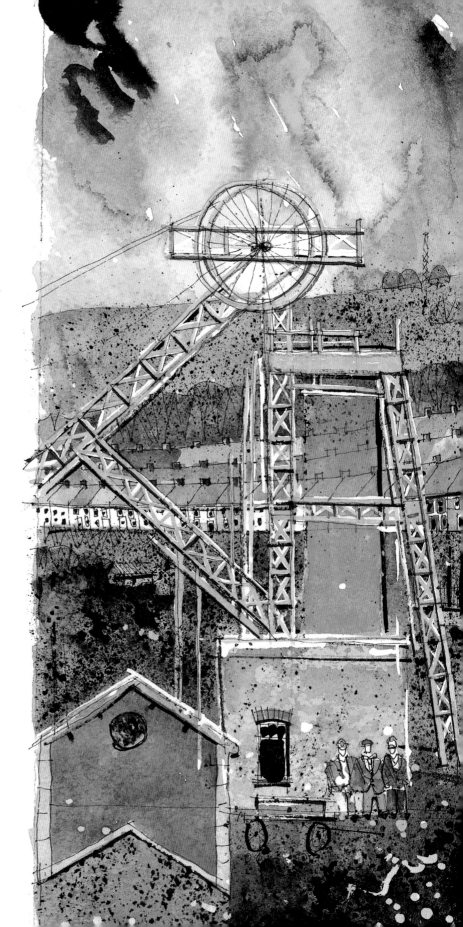

RHONDDA: MINESHAFT
In the 19th century the Welsh
valleys North of Cardiff were
developed for coal mining on a
huge scale. At first, separate
villages appeared, but they soon
expanded, and each settlement
merged into the next, forming
ribbon development on the
lower slopes for the full length
of the valleys.

Mining is no longer the major
industry it used to be, and gradually the industrial landscape is
being tidied up and returned to
nature: in the Rhondda, the most
famous of mining valleys, a
heritage centre is being established, to make sure that this
unique environment, and the
sacrifices made by so many, are
not forgotten.

UFFCULME: COLDHARBOUR MILL

Ever since the Middle Ages, Devon had a flourishing woollen industry, partly because of its lush
pastures, and this continued into the 17th and 18th
centuries.

An example of the architectural consequences
of this can be seen at Uffculme. In 1788 a new mill
was built on the River Culm, and in 1797 it was
bought by Sir Thomas Fox, for producing cloth.
Steam power was introduced in 1865, and a
branch railway arrived in 1876. Local houses were
built for the mill workers. Today it is a working
wool museum, still operational.

Farming

Agricultural buildings are similar to industrial buildings, in that their form can be seen to follow their function. They represent an aspect of architecture which is now far better understood than it was just a couple of decades ago.

It is curious that agricultural buildings can vary so much in sensitivity to their surroundings. Buildings like wind and tidemills are utterly dependant upon and entwined with nature, and their design has to relate completely to the natural forces which they utilize. By contrast much of our countryside is covered by ugly Dutch barns and silos built of profiled metal sheeting, which, for reasons I do not understand, are outside the control of the town and country planning legislation.

EAST RIDDLESDEN HALL TITHE BARN

This is one of the country's finest tithe barns. These were built to provide storage for the tithe: a 10 per cent tax of produce from the land, paid by tenants to their landlord.

Surpassed in scale only by castles, cathedrals and churches, tithe barns had close similarities with religious buildings, with a central nave and side aisles, and magnificent timber roof structures.

East Riddlesden tithe barn is 120 feet long and 80 feet wide. It has eight structural bays, and there are arched porches over huge side doorways which, in addition to providing access, also allowed through the breezes to separate the straw and chaff from the grain.

SWALEDALE: FIELD BARNS

Swaledale is a majestic and wide U-shaped glacial valley. The lower slopes are fertile and have been subdivided into countless small fields, which tend to have their longest side running across the valley. Many of these fields have their own barns, and the position of these vary: sometimes they stand in the middle of the field, and elsewhere they are in a corner or built along one edge. The isolated nature of the barns is emphasized by the tightly-packed character of Yorkshire villages, with the houses clustered together for shelter.

The reason for these 'field barns' is to minimize the number of journeys back to the main farm buildings. They provide shelter for cattle and storage space for hay. Often they were built into the hillside to provide access at two levels: to cattle on the lower floor and hay on the upper.

The walls dividing the barns from the field are carboniferous limestone, a local material, and the barns are simple and practical constructions. The barn walls are of inner and outer skins of stone, with the core filled with rubble. Larger stones, taken right through the wall to bind it together, project from the outside face of the barn wall.

WILLINGTON DOVECOTE

Willington is a few miles outside Bedford. It boasts a fabulous dovecote built in the middle of the 16th century. Nearby Newnham Priory had been dissolved, and provided the secondhand stone.

Dovecotes are generally much smaller, circular buildings. This spectacular effort provides nesting for about 1500 birds, which fly in through the slats between the two roof sections.

CRANBROOK WINDMILL

Cranbrook was once a major and wealthy town, gaining its prosperity from the cloth industry. Its pretty weatherboarded cottages are dominated by a fine windmill, still in working order.

Built in 1814, the mill has a generous brick base which raises it up above the level of the houses to catch the wind. The white timber cladding fans out at the bottom, like a smock.

SAXTED GREEN MILL ➤

At the lowest level of this mill there is a round house, containing the mill stones. Above this, clad in white weatherboarding, is the main body of the building, housing the main mechanism. The fantail at the rear automatically turns the mill to face the prevailing wind. Still in working order, the mill is run by English Heritage, and is open to the public in the summer.

◄ WOODBRIDGE TIDEMILL

Mills for grinding corn were commonplace buildings, utilizing the force of the wind or a fast-flowing stream. This mill at Woodbridge is unusual in that it used the incoming tide to fill a pond with water, and when the sea level dropped, this water would be released to fall under gravity and thereby drive the mill mechanism. The main disadvantage, of course, was the intermittent nature of the supply, but nevertheless it was a clever use of a natural resource.

Marine

By definition, nautical buildings occupy some of the most extreme and inclement locations in Britain. The architecture is therefore suitably robust and functional. This leads to a distinct and attractive architectural language of brightly-coloured lighthouses, seats, railings and cafes, and solid, rugged quaysides.

HASTINGS: NET HOUSES

These 43 peculiarly-shaped constructions are fishermen's net houses, positioned under the East Hill at Hastings and thought to have been built early last century. Once there were roughly 110. Some were destroyed or damaged by fire in 1961; all that were left were restored between 1985-91.

Used to store nets and ropes which would rot if not hung up to dry, the huts measure about 13 feet by 13 feet. Their shape evolved to avoid taking up too much space on the beach.

CHATHAM: BOLLARD

There is a whole kit of nautical
paraphernalia: railings, bollards,
buoys, signal masts, lighthouses,
quay walls, steps, seats ...

They form a harmonious
group and, simple, functional
and uncompromising, they have
to withstand repeated use and
frightening weather. Somehow
though, perhaps through the use
of bright colours, or because of
the seaside association, they
combine their solid dependa-
bility with a bright jollity.

NASHPOINT LIGHTHOUSE

This lighthouse was built in 1832. At first there was
only one bungalow; the second was added twenty
years later.

The bungalows are square in plan, with a room
in each corner. A chimney at the centre provides a
fireplace to every room; it is a neat and economic
arrangement. A corridor links the living area to the
circular lighthouse.

The lighthouse is squat and unspectacular; the
whole group is compact, functional and utilitarian.

LIVERPOOL: PUMP STATION

The docks at Liverpool are no longer used for the purpose for which they were built; instead they are now a major tourist attraction. With some clever conversions many of the warehouses have found alternative uses as restaurants, shops and galleries. This old pump station, and the quayside, with its paving and bits of old machinery, all provide a fascinating area in which to wander.

Unfortunately tourism provides only a fraction of the employment of the old dockyards. One does not have to travel far inland from the docks to find the dereliction, vandalism and despondency which decaying industry brings.

LONGSTONE LIGHTHOUSE

Longstone Lighthouse of the Farne Islands is offshore from Bamburgh, on the Northumbrian coast. It is just the sort of image we think of when imagining a lighthouse, the bold horizontal panels of red and white making a stark contrast with the irregular and menacing form of the rocks upon which it has been built.

Leisure

Since the last war there has been a dramatic increase in the leisure time available to people. This has led to the wide range of leisure buildings: sports halls, squash courts, swimming pools, galleries, wine bars, museums and so on. Conversely, multi-ownership of televisions and video recorders has caused the closure of mass entertainment venues like cinemas and music halls. Overall, this is a rapidly changing type of building, constantly updating with new fashions and technology.

BUXTON

Buxton does not quite match Bath or Edinburgh in the quality or quantity of its Georgian architecture, but it does come close. The town spa was discovered by the Romans, but was not exploited until the end of the 18th century when Buxton became a Midlands competitor to Bath.

The 5th Duke of Devonshire promoted the town and built its finest building, the Crescent.

Lamentably, this magnificent structure became derelict in 1991, and when I visited it the following year the windows were boarded up, the roof was letting in the rain, rot was taking hold, and untold damage was being caused.

Modern imitations of Georgian buildings are being built all over the country, while one of the finest examples of the real thing is rotting away.

ABERYSTWYTH

In the last century the theory was promoted that bathing in sea water was of medicinal benefit. Great promenades were built along the sea front, lined by terraces of guest houses and hotels. Aberystwyth, halfway down the West coast of Wales, is a typical example of such a seaside resort.

The buildings are on a grand scale, sweeping terraces of three storeys and more. Windows project out to maximize the view, and the detailing of the buildings is decorative, even frivolous. The facades are brightly painted, white with touches of pink, yellow or blue, sparkling in the sunlight.

ELGAR'S BIRTHPLACE

Shortly before his death in 1934, Sir Edward Elgar told his daughter that if there was ever a museum established to commemorate his life and work, he would like it to be in the tiny labourer's cottage where he was born, in Great Malvern.

This has created a problem: the number of visitors, and the attendant need for parking, shopping, refreshments and lavatories, has totally changed the idyllic character, so cherished by Elgar, of this corner of the country. A proposed new visitors' centre is currently the subject of a big planning dispute.

ANNE HATHAWAY'S COTTAGE

Anne Hathaway's cottage is the most attractive of the popular 'Shakespeare sites'. Located in a village, Shottery, to the West of Stratford-on-Avon, it is where Shakespeare's wife spent her childhood. Built in the 15th century, it is of timber-framed construction with wattle and daub infill. The interior has much of the original furniture. Visit out of season if you want to see anything other than fellow tourists.

THOMAS HARDY'S HOME

Thomas Hardy's birthplace in Higher Bockhampton, Dorset, challenges Anne Hathaway's cottage as a candidate for the chocolate boxes. The cottage was built in 1801 by Hardy's great grandfather. His father was a master builder, and Hardy himself studied architecture before turning to writing.

BRIGHTON: ROYAL PAVILION

Brighton is Britain's most famous resort, and nothing captures the seaside spirit better than the Royal Pavilion. Hopelessly impractical in its extraordinary forms, which are virtually impossible to maintain, it is hideous yet frivolous. The inspiration behind the building was the Prince Regent, later George IV.

Royalty had helped the development of Brighton and other seaside resorts, by supporting the theory that sea water had medicinal value and that bathing in it would therefore be beneficial. Weymouth was more popular at first, but Brighton grew more quickly through its easy access to and from London, and became more spectacular. In 1841 the railway connected Brighton to the capital, and its popularity grew still further.

Before all this, Brighton had been a small fishing port. Its old cobbled streets, 'the Lanes', are now quaint little alleys, housing souvenir shops and attracting tourists.

BURY ST EDMUNDS: THE NUTSHELL

The Nutshell is a typically reticent building. With maximum dimensions of just sixteen foot by seven foot six inches, it claims to be the smallest pub in the country. I have no idea whether this is true, although I can confirm that the beer it serves is very satisfactory.

LUDLOW: THE FEATHERS

This was once a private house, and dates back to 1603. It became an inn in the middle of the 17th century. The upper levels cantilever out over the street, and the whole building is a celebration of decorative timberwork. The detailed leadwork for the windows is in the same spirit. The overall effect is enhanced by the colour of the timbers, a silvery greenish grey.

GLASGOW: THE BURRELL GALLERY

The distinctive feature of this building is its siting, in a park, yet not far from the centre of Glasgow. This has been exploited fully by glazing the North wall of the building closest to the trees, giving a constant source of reference and relief for the visitor.

The architectural style of the building is simple and understated, so one's attention is drawn to the collection. A building as restrained as this actually requires considerable skill and ingenuity to achieve, and is a work of art in itself.

LORD'S CRICKET GROUND: THE MOUND STAND

This is the sort of contemporary architecture we should aim to produce. The building ties in with its surroundings, with massive brick arches facing on to St John's Wood Road. Above this is a lightweight tent structure, supported on six huge masts. It is like a vast marquee, and entirely appropriate for lazy afternoons watching cricket.

The curve of the stand has been exploited with the series of tent roofs, stepping up and down, creating a most interesting composition, whilst elements like the scoreboard and the clock are both modern and appropriate.

SOUTHGATE: ROYAL BIRKDALE LINKS

Success in sport is momentary; for a few days an athlete enjoys unprecedented success, and is a star. A major event arrives in town, and the place is submerged by spectators and the media.

Royal Birkdale is a links golf course used for the Open Championship in 1991. Suddenly, the pavilion was seen on our television screens as a backdrop to the world's leading players. Then, the event concluded, the pavilion reverted to its true status: a rather plain and ordinary building.

Education

Education buildings shape our lives: after the home, the first building with which many of us associate closely is our school.

Although schools share the same function, their buildings vary greatly, from big draughty Victorian halls to modern prefabs with leaky flat roofs. The scale is diverse too, from the small village school to complete university complexes.

EWELME

This is an enchanting group of buildings, built between 1434-36 by William de la Pole, Duke of Suffolk, in the grounds of his manor house.

The setting is beautiful: country lanes, barns, a stream and village cottages. Approaching the group, the school is seen first, rising out of a bank above the roadway. Beyond this are almshouses, gathered around a small cloistered courtyard. Then, up some steps, is the church. This is built of flint and stone, while the school and almshouses are mostly brick and wood. The group has an almost monastic sense of seclusion and calm.

MANCHESTER UNIVERSITY

Until the 19th century, Oxford and Cambridge were the only universities in England. Then came the foundation of London University, and the great civic universities, such as Leeds, Liverpool, Birmingham and Manchester.

Local support from wealthy businessmen played an important part in this, and a good deal of pride was at stake as well. Just as town halls were in part status symbols (see pages 56-7), the same applied to the main offices and function rooms of the new universities. Manchester University turned to Sir Alfred Waterhouse to design its main centrepiece building; he also designed Manchester's town hall (see page 57).

CAMBRIDGE: KING'S COLLEGE

In Cambridge, the richness of the townscape relies
upon contrast, particularly between the scale and
style of the architecture of the gown, which
balances that of the town.

The East side of King's College is formed by a
screenway and entrance gatehouse which were
designed by William Wilkins and built between
1824 and 1828. It is a grand and impressive
statement, and contrasts nicely with the smaller
scale and varied buildings on the opposite side of
King's Parade (see book jacket).

ETON COLLEGE

Eton College was founded by Henry VI in 1442. Its buildings are arranged around courtyards, very similar to the Oxford and Cambridge colleges.

Whatever one thinks of Eton as an educational establishment, there can be no doubt about the quality of its architecture. Distant views, like that from Windsor for example, are dominated by the long form and the pinnacles of the chapel.

Residential

A study of residential buildings is as much a study of Britain's social history as an architectural analysis. From castles for monarchs and lord of the manor residences to farm workers' cottages and mining town terraces, the range is immense in terms of setting, scale, style and detail.

KEDLESTON HALL

Begun in 1759, Kedleston Hall in Derbyshire is the result of a close collaboration between the client, Sir Nathaniel Curzon (whose family has lived here since the 12th century), and his architect, Robert Adam.

Kedleston is the most complete example of Adam's work. There is a main central block, with lower wings on either side linked by curved corridors which sweep forward to embrace the visitor on arrival. This arrangement was planned, but not executed, on the South side, leaving a less formal relationship there with the hill beyond.

The church to the West of the house is all that remains of Kedleston village which used to be here; it was later rebuilt beyond the West boundary of the estate.

HADDON HALL

This medieval manor house is set on a slope above Derbyshire's River Wye in glorious pastoral limestone scenery. It dates from Norman times and consists of various buildings including an entrance gateway, chapel, banqueting hall, clock tower, kitchens, bedrooms, and a long gallery. This accommodation is arranged around two courtyards, linked by a passageway.

The whole composition is unified by the use of the same material – stone – and through the courtyard design. The Oxford and Cambridge college quadrangles, which were built later, are remarkably similar.

The gardens are attractively laid out as a series of terraces. The main entrance to the manor house is unusually positioned in one corner of the lower courtyard, approached up some steps.

AMBLESIDE
Was this built for fun, or was it a
clever way of saving money?
Perhaps the site it was built on
was free because no one
actually owned it.

In this past decade we have
tried similar tricks, on a larger
scale, building shopping centres
over motorways and offices
above railway tracks.

WHALLEY

These estate workers' cottages along the River Ribble were erected in about 1830. The white walls and Gothic arched windows are distinctive, making the little group stand out from the hillside.

ASKHAM

Askham has a liking for red. Most of the village is black, grey and white, but little touches of red paint here and there, bring the whole place to life.

Little alleys between the houses allowed the villagers to bring the cattle into the centre of the settlement if the Scots launched an attack.

The arrangement of houses on either side of a broad central green is very typical of Yorkshire.

SIDMOUTH

In the late 18th and early 19th centuries, Sidmouth became a very popular seaside retreat, attracting royalty and nobility. Romantic country cottages were built to accommodate them.

The cottage illustrated once had a thatched roof. This was replaced by expensive hexagonal tiles in the middle of the 19th century. The pink walls are quite startling.

By the second half of the 19th century Sidmouth was past its peak. It remains a thoroughly civilized place, much admired by the retired.

MILBURN

This is residential and agricultural architecture entwined. A single form is divided into a home for the farmer and his family, and the cattle shed. The two are differentiated by changes in materials. One could argue that the red Triassic sandstone for the cows is superior to the walls of the house.

ALMSHOUSES, ABINGDON

A few minutes walk from the centre of Abingdon there is the church of St Helen's. In its churchyard there are three groups of almshouses built to house the poor. Long Alley almshouses were built in 1446; the timber cloister was added in 1500. Twitty's almshouses were constructed in 1706, and Brick Alley almshouses twelve years later. Together they form a secluded and pleasant place to live.

OTHAM: WEALDEN HOUSE

Wealden houses were built from the 14th to the 16th century by wealthy farmers. Found throughout Southeast England, they were especially common in the weald of Kent and Sussex.

The name was given to a particular form and layout of house which was so successful it was used again and again. Based on a simple rectangular shape, the two ends are of two storeys, while the middle comprises a double-height main hall with an open fireplace. The upper levels project forward slightly at the front, creating a recess with deep overhanging eaves at the centre.

Curved struts support the eaves, the decoration is quite restrained. Roofs are usually steeply pitched, and walls are timber framed with closely spaced vertical members, and infilled with wattle and daub or herringbone brickwork. This house at Otham in Kent is a characteristic example.

CROSSGATES

The original house was minute,
one room downstairs and
another upstairs. Various bits
have been added, using
economical materials.

LLANRHIAN

In the Pembrokeshire Coast National Park there
are many cottages like this. The layout was simple:
a central door off the road provided access to the
hall with rooms opening off on either side. These
had chimneys on their outside end walls. A ladder
led up to the first floor which had bedrooms on
either side. The dormer windows were added later;
originally just the gable window let in light.

The lower floors were simply flattened earth,
and before the windows were glazed, shutters
kept out the wind and rain. The roof has been
cemented over and lime washed as extra protection. The cottage is dug deep into the hillside; the
winter weather can be fierce in this exposed area.

BARRA

Crofts are smallholdings of a few
acres in the Scottish Highlands.
Generally they support sheep
farming, and the crofter often
turns his hand to other activities
such as fishing or building.

  Croft-houses like this one at
Barra are of simple and robust
construction. The walls are thick,
built of large stones, and the
roof is thatched. A small hole
allows smoke, from peat fires, to
escape through the roof. Not so
long ago livestock shared the
dwelling, with the floor sloped
to carry their effluent out of the
building through low-level holes.

TELEGRAPH HILL

Victorian suburbs grew up around railway stations. After a period of decline they are much sought after again, people recognizing that spatially they are more generous than later styles.

These houses could be almost anywhere, but are in Telegraph Hill in Southeast London. There are many variations in detail but really they are just variations on a theme. The general layout is so effective; it gives good light to the living areas, allows for changes in level, minimizes circulation, and is easily roofed.

External features include a recessed porch, bay windows, stained glass, brick elevations with stone features, and low, pitched Welsh slate roofs.

LLANFYLLIN

Built in the early 19th century and of timber-framed construction, this terrace is quite attractive, but is very basic. Originally there was a single room on each floor, with a large open fire on the ground level and just a ladder providing access to the upper storey.

STAPLEFORD
Very similar to North Street in Cromford, 'two-up, two-down' living spaces had a floor on top for knitting or weaving, well lit by strip windows. Sometimes the party walls were omitted on the second floor to create a large communal workspace.

MANCHESTER
Some Victorian housing was too dense, with little daylight or ventilation, and minimal sanitation. Typical examples can be seen in Manchester; row upon row of long parallel streets, their width controlled through bylaws. Cross streets run at right angles to the main streets, and between the terraces are narrow alleys.

The houses have backyards, which originally contained an outside lavatory, and were used for hanging washing to dry and for the collection of rubbish. The houses were often built right on to the pavement, and the entrance sometimes leads straight into the front room.

Bay windows and decorative stone or terracotta features provide variety and indicate slightly grander dwellings.

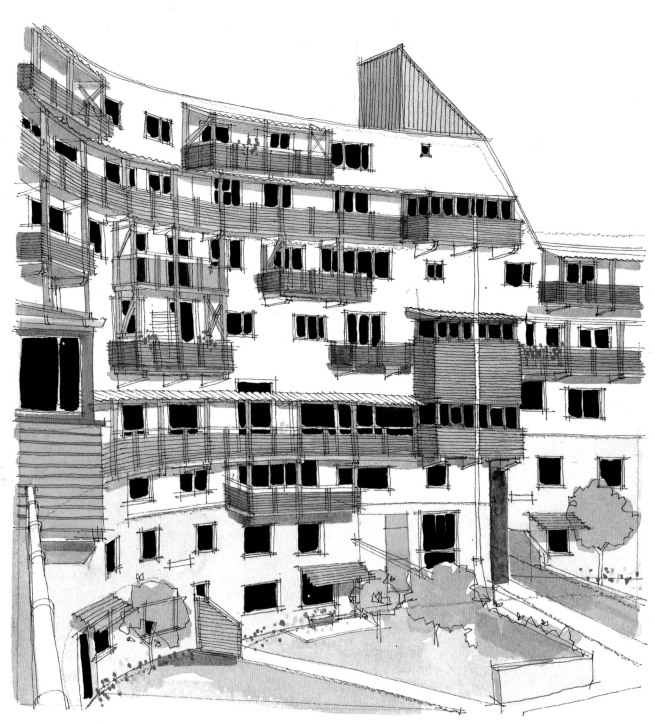

BYKER WALL

Started in the late 1960s, this scheme represents a more humane approach to rehousing large numbers of people than most slum clearance schemes. The local community was closely consulted as the design developed.

The result is a building of two main sides. The North face is plain and austere; it faces the road and metro train line, and contains bathrooms and kitchens. The South elevation has the living accommodation and overlooks playgrounds and gardens. Colourful balconies project out. It is lively, fun and individual.

BUILDING MATERIALS, DECORATION AND DETAIL

THE DETAILS OF OUR SURROUNDINGS matter a great deal. Frequently we are as aware of the details as we are of the broader overall picture: they are what we come into immediate contact with – the doorway through which we enter; the windows we open; the handrails and ironmongery we touch; the signs we read; the colours, textures and decoration we enjoy looking at.

Details and decoration are at their best when they are clearly – and perhaps cleverly – derived from functional necessity. Gargoyles are ornate and amusing features, but their original purpose was to throw rainwater off a roof. Decorative stone drip mouldings break up large expanses of brickwork, and also protect the brick face from water running down the facade.

Historically, people invested much time in attending to the details of a building, with craftsmen producing individual carvings in brick and stone, or fancy brickwork or roof coverings.

This craftsmanship is still available. You can get stone beautifully carved today, just as it used to be, but it is extremely expensive for building contractors to train and keep craftsmen who may not be fully engaged at all times.

Interesting detail is not the unique preserve of older trades and natural materials. Modern buildings can have great elegance and richness of detail too, and, to be successful, this would be derived from necessity. Too often decoration and detail is applied whimsically. This is not to deny the elaboration of high Gothic or baroque, nor the modern equivalents. The problem is where the detail is quite simply unnecessary.

SEVENOAKS

The market square in Sevenoaks is surrounded by buildings of a pleasing mixture of heights, styles, and materials. Brick, Kentish ragstone, pegtiles, slate, timber with plaster infill, tile hanging and mathematical tiles are all used. There are medieval buildings, as well as Gothic and classical. There is richness in the detailing, with decorative plaster, timber and brickwork.

It is a space typical of many towns, having evolved by chance in response to various forces including land ownership, topography, use for outside activities, and the need for enclosure. Many of the components, which together make up buildings and spaces, can be seen here. Places like this can be improved dramatically, by altering the paving, signage, shopfronts, lighting, planting, market stalls, security systems, aerials, and so on. These details matter.

ILLUSTRATION PAGE 105:
Saffron Walden: Window

Stone

Stone is much sought after, the most noble of building materials. However, it is expensive, especially when imported from outside a region, and its weathering and 'hardwearing' qualities are sometimes overrated.

The finest stone is from a belt of Jurassic stone running diagonally across England, from Lincoln, through Northamptonshire, Oxfordshire and the Cotswolds, and into Somerset. The colour of the stone varies, but usually it is of a gorgeous, warm golden hue. Because many villages had their own local quarry, the stone buildings blend with their settings almost as though they have been hewn from the hillside.

There are other building stones, varying from the warm, red Triassic sandstones, of variable quality, to the hard, grey carboniferous limestone and millstone grit found in the Pennines.

LINCOLN: JEW'S HOUSE,
In the past Lincoln has had a large and flourishing Jewish community. The Jew's House was built in the 12th century and is one of the oldest domestic buildings in Britain still in use.

CHIPPING CAMPDEN

The Cotswolds have the village showpieces of Britain: prim, proper, and rather self-satisfied.

The villages made their wealth between the 15th to 18th centuries from sheep farming, and they were also blessed with beautiful local stone in a creamy, golden hue. We are the benefactors of this: an abundance of churches, manor houses, cottages, market halls and even garden walls all built in the lovely stone, with huge variations in style and detail.

The villages became popular at the end of the 19th century, when people began to appreciate the rolling countryside and charming villages.

Gradually properties were gentrified, and the area now suffers through proximity to London, which makes it an ideal location for a holiday cottage.

The use and beauty of stone as a roof covering is perhaps not fully appreciated. Some stones laminate easily into thin sheets through frost action. These are ideal for roofing, with larger stones being laid at the eaves and diminishing courses of smaller stones up to the ridge. To shed any rain quickly roofs are very steeply pitched. Sometimes the weight of the stones has caused the roofs to sag in the middle, which only adds to the quaint and aged appearance.

WELLS: VICAR'S CLOSE
Until the 15th century stone was
precious and its use largely
limited to cathedrals, churches
and castles, except in areas
where abundant stone was
readily available. Gradually it
became used for buildings
associated with religious use,
such as Bishops' palaces,
rectories, and buildings like
Vicar's Close in Wells. In the
shadow of the cathedral itself,
two parallel terraces of houses
with spectacular chimney stacks
line the close. The road has
wide drainage channels at its
edges, which are bridged by
huge slabs of stone.

BIBURY

Arlington Row in Bibury was built by Augustine Friars in 1360. Originally for storage, the buildings were only converted into cottages in the 17th century.

These buildings have taken on their present appearance over a long period of time – a settlement of the ground here, a rotten roof timber there ... all contribute to the well-worn, slightly tumbledown character. It would not be possible to recreate this, and even if it were, it would be contrived; and this is why Arlington Row, and others like it, are so cherished. William Morris certainly appreciated it, describing Bibury as 'the most beautiful village in England'.

WEST YORKSHIRE: COTTAGE

Although Yorkshire's farmhouses are built using the same material as the Cotswold showpieces, the stone used is of a very different type. It is carboniferous limestone, grey, hard, rough-textured and difficult to carve.

The farmhouses are straightforward, tough and with nothing fancy about them. In the villages, houses huddle closely together to keep out the cold winds; isolated farmhouses sit as low as they possibly can.

Granite

Granite is an igneous rock; tough, impervious and durable. Very precise and fine jointing can be achieved, and granite can also take a high polish. Its appearance can be rather dull and uniform, although it sparkles and comes to life after rainfall.

ABERDEEN: GRANITE CITY

In Aberdeen, not only the grand public buildings were constructed of locally-quarried granite but also ordinary houses and tenements; Aberdeen is known deservedly as the Granite City.

The stone is usually blue-grey in colour although there are variations, such as a touch of pink, which helps relieve what would otherwise be a rather oppressive material when its use is so widespread.

CASTLE DROGO

Dramatically sited high about the Teign Valley, Castle Drogo is built of exquisitely shaped and cut granite. It is like a fortress, with the entrance tower having turrets and a portcullis. At the rear of the house the character alters, with large windows.

Inside granite is used for lintels over doorways and fireplaces; the doors are timber, a lovely contrast. The backstage areas are fascinating, with precise detailing of timber stairs, worktops and storage racks. Even here granite is everywhere.

Slate

Slate is a metamorphic rock, and varies a good deal in colour and texture. It is extremely hard but very brittle. It has a closed texture and is impervious, making it an ideal roofing material.

Lakeland slate is often split thicker and rougher than Welsh slate. It also has more colour variation, and is therefore more characterful than the Welsh.

CADER IDRIS: COTTAGE
As slate is a material which can be split quite easily, it is suitable for flooring, steps, shelves, windowsills, copings, damp proof courses and, of course, roofs.

Traditionally the courses of a roof are graded from about 24 inches at the eaves, to just six inches below the ridge. The slates are double lapped so half of the length of a slate is invisible. These roofs weigh a considerable amount, so if any of the supporting timberwork is undersized or has suffered rot or insect attack, then the roof soon starts to bow under the strain.

Flint

This is a curious material, extremely hard but easily fractured. It is most commonly found in East Anglia and the Southeast, and has been widely used in many of the finest churches in East Anglia (see Lavenham, page 46).

Initially the flints were simply laid at random with lots of mortar, but used in this way it is a dull and mundane material. Regular courses of flint appeared after about 1250, and this gives a more ordered and attractive appearance.

The material is seen at its best when the flints are split and built into the wall with the fractured face showing; these are known as knapped flints. Flushwork describes the decorative use of flint with stone used at corners, window and door surrounds, and other details with which flint cannot cope.

A good time to see flint buildings is in sunlight after a shower which has freshened the split face of the flint and made it sparkle.

HAMBLEDON
This is a sleepy little village in Buckinghamshire. I visited one summer Friday afternoon and the only sound was a tractor cutting the outfield, ready for the weekend cricket.

The deep green of the lush grass and trees complements the rich red brickwork and tiles. The greens and reds are of a similar tone which accentuates the lively colour of the flintwork.

Brick

Bricks were first introduced to Britain by the Romans, and at the end of the Middle Ages were imported from the Low Countries. They first became popular in the parts of Britain nearest to the Continent, before spreading North and West.

The colours and textures vary widely, from the deep reds of Hampshire and the Thames valley, to the pale buffs and yellows of East Anglia. Bricks were generally made from local clay, thereby helping to integrate buildings and landscape.

Good quality bricks are very durable, yet mellow attractively with age. Brick also lends itself to an immense variety of ornamentation and pattern making. The ends of bricks, or 'headers', are closest to the heat in the kiln, which vitrifies them to contrast in colour with the rest of the brick. This can be exploited to make patterns where the headers can be seen.

Bricks resist heat very effectively, better than stone. Chimneys have commonly been built of brick, and fancy and decorative chimneystacks are a common feature of British buildings.

BLANDFORD FORUM

Over a period of just 30 years, Blandford Forum, a wealthy market town, was completely rebuilt following a major fire in 1731. The rebuilding was mostly carried out by local master builders.

Most buildings were rebuilt in red brick, with feature courses in grey, and some decorative stonework. The style is mainly Georgian, and the result is handsome, if lacking some variety.

The original street pattern was kept, just as in the City of London after the Great Fire, demonstrating that once established, street layouts were not generally changed.

Terracotta

Very fine sand and clay is used to form this tile-like material, literally 'cooked earth'. Cheaper than stone, it is a good material to use for decorative detail. Reasonably resistant to weathering, the major problem is that the material shrinks on firing, making dimensional accuracy difficult to achieve, although this can be overcome by keeping the components quite small.

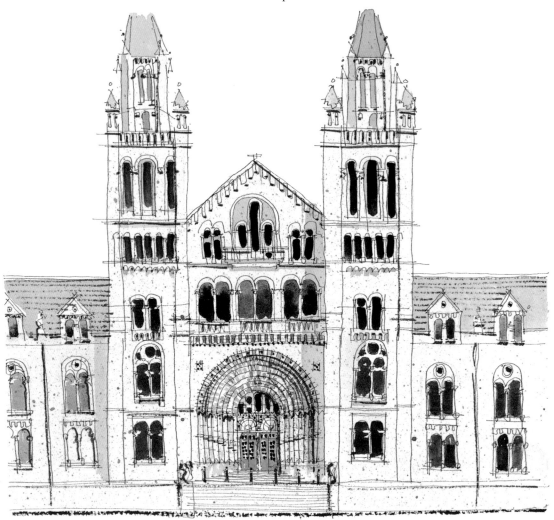

NATURAL HISTORY MUSEUM

Built between 1873-80, the Natural History Museum is a monumental building. The main entrance has a huge porch leading into a big space, like the nave of a church, with an iron roof above.

There are wings on either side of the entrance which creates a most impressive facade. Terracotta, in subtle blues and creams, and with intricate detailing, is widely used. The architectural treatment has great empathy with a museum of natural history.

Cob & Thatch

Thatch – straw, reed or heather – is the lightest of roofing materials, and is therefore the most appropriate to use with walls of low load-bearing capacity, such as cob.

Cob is a mixture of wet earth, straw, gravel and sand. When lime is added to the mix it sets hard. It was built up in layers, each being allowed to dry thoroughly before the next was added.

Thatch is common in East Anglia where it works well with coloured plastered walls (see Clare, page 123), while the thatch and cob combination is best seen in Dorset and Devon.

BROADHEMBURY

Virtually every building in Broadhembury is built of cob and thatch. The thatched roofs exhibit all the characteristic features of this material: no gutter is provided, with the roof simply having a deep overhang at the eaves; the eaves-line is broken by windows which create the quaint undulating roof-edge; at the ridge, where extra protection is needed, straw is simply bent over the ridge, and the lower edges shaped decoratively.

Similarly, cob has evolved a series of details which have arisen from necessity. Cob needs to be kept off the ground and so was often built off a brick or stone plinth; extra resistance was often achieved by painting this with tar.

Timber

Much larger areas of Britain used to be covered by forests. A large proportion of this was hardwood, particularly oak, a timber of great strength and durability. Britain's buildings have benefited greatly from this natural resource. But timber is vulnerable to rot, woodworm and fire, and sadly the stock of timber-framed buildings of today are only a fraction of the original.

Many regional variations evolved: square panels and the use of tar to blacken the timbers characterize the West Midlands, while in East Anglia closely-spaced verticals are common. Overhanging upper floors became very popular; this has a practical benefit as the floor beams are less likely to sag in the middle, and the projecting bays provide protection to the walls below. The gain in floor space and the picturesque appearance were incidental advantages.

CRANBROOK

Cranbrook is an attractive, quiet village. This belies its past because it was once the centre of cloth manufacture in the Weald. Its heyday was from the 14th to the 18th century, but when its industry declined so did its importance.

It is a charming place with old houses built right on the edge of the street, giving an impression of intimacy without claustrophobia; the white horizontal boarding of many of the houses ensures that this is the case.

CHATHAM: UPPER MAST HOUSE

The dockyard at Chatham opened in 1547, and after 400 years use, closed in 1984.

About 40-50 buildings are still there, and it is a thriving tourist attraction. The buildings are mostly simple and functional, and all the more elegant for that. There is the ropery, the mast house and the timber-seasoning sheds – a mixture of uses for great purpose-made timber constructions.

LAVENHAM GUILDHALL

When the Guildhall was built in 1529, Lavenham was at its pinnacle. It became wealthy through the wool trade in the 14th and 15th centuries, and the church is another fine building which demonstrates the success of the village, with its 14th-century tower of knapped flint (see page 46).

At one time the Guildhall was the town's gaol, but it has since been restored and is now owned by the National Trust. The timberwork has been left unpainted, and most of the timbers are closely spaced and vertical. The Guildhall dominates the market square, and while other buildings in the village are smaller, together they represent a prime selection of timber-framed buildings.

DIDBROOK

This is an excellent example of a cruck frame, which was widely used in the West Midlands and the North. The principles of this construction are straightforward: each frame is made by inclining two lengths of timber to meet at the top, making a shape like a tent. If curved timbers are chosen, more headroom can be created under them.

The cruck frames are repeated at intervals and purlins span longitudinally between them. They support rafters and then the roof covering, which would commonly have been thatch. The whole thing is like an upturned boat.

WEOBLEY

Timber framing in Herefordshire was very common, right up until the Industrial Revolution. The Ley in Weobley is a fine old farmhouse, dated 1589. The oak framing, left in its natural state, has weathered to a lovely, shiny, silvery, colour, much more attractive than the usual black paint.

The subdivision into square panels was characteristic of this part of the country, although the understated decorative detail is less elaborate than the ornamentation usually found here.

Stucco, Plastering & Pargetting

Plastering the outside of a building provides an extra protective layer and also a smooth finish. Pargetting is the process of introducing ornamental designs into the plasterwork, either by cutting into the surface or by raising it in relief.

Stucco includes cement, and is made as smooth and hard as possible. Lines are incised into it to simulate stone coursing, and then it is painted.

SAFFRON WALDEN
Saffron Walden expanded to become a wealthy town in the Middle Ages (see page 131). Many of its buildings are timber-framed, often covered by plaster and then painted. The finish is rarely perfect but it does provide a pleasant contrast with the rougher textures and varied colours of other materials.

DORSET SQUARE

Dorset Square was conceived as a whole (see page 36), and is an exemplary use of stucco, which became very popular in London in the late 18th century in areas like Belgravia, Kensington and Pimlico. Its use was copied in spa towns such as Tunbridge Wells and Cheltenham.

Hard, crisp and clean, the material oozes class; the fact that it requires repeated redecoration simply adds to the sense of indulgence.

CLARE

Plastering then painting gives the option of choosing any colour you like. There is little point in painting your house the colour of brick, wood or stone; to do so would be to deny the intrinsic choice presented by plaster and paint. Equally, too vivid a colour would seem unnatural and out of keeping with other building materials.

These cottages on the green at Clare strike the perfect balance: a pastel pink that is eye-catching but not overbearing.

During the Middle Ages Britain imported its best glass from the Continent, and until the 16th century glass for windows remained a luxury, and most had wooden shutters instead.

The number of windows became a measure of wealth, and the window tax was introduced in 1696, leading to the widespread blocking up of windows. The Act was repealed in 1851, shortly after the first sheet glass was manufactured in 1838, and since then it has been possible to create larger and larger windows. While this can be used to good effect to allow light into interiors and to visually link the inside and outside, large windows with no subdivision can look crude and out of scale in certain surroundings.

Glass

SALTAIRE: WINDOW DETAIL
This is one of the larger houses in Saltaire (see page 27) although even the smallest, simplest dwellings were given some decoration. Here it is taken further and the window has been subdivided by the leadwork to make an attractive geometric pattern.

CHATSWORTH: CONSERVATIVE WALL

Joseph Paxton was appointed head gardener at Chatsworth in 1826, and in 1848 he completed his 'conservative wall'. This is on the South side of the garden wall which runs between the house and the stable block, to form a thin, long building of over 300 feet in length. The hillside is quite steep, and the building steps up with it. Some of the plants are as old as the building.

It has regular narrow vertical panes, a tall central section with five bays on either side, and an attractive fanlight over the central door. The building is simple but very elegant.

KEW: TEMPERATE HOUSE

Designed by Decimus Burton and built between 1844-8, this was the world's biggest glass house when it was completed.

A bold and innovative construction, the skeleton consists of a series of identical cast iron ribs. A lighter tracery of elements is above, carrying all the panes of glass. Restored in 1982, the building retains an airy, mystical quality.

Concrete is a much maligned material, often associated with 'concrete jungles' or leaking flat roofs. In fact it is a wonderfully flexible material, capable of being formed into almost any shape and able to create very thin and elegant structures. The finished appearance can be very fine, with a wide range of textures, from smoothly polished to a rough, hammered look.

Concrete never looks good when wet, but this can be overcome by careful control of where the rainwater goes. It is all a question of how well the material is designed and whether the budget is sufficient to use the material as it should be used.

Concrete

THE THAMES BARRIER
Opened in 1984, this is a remarkable engineering concept and achievement. A series of huge plates lie flat most of the time but can swing up into place to prevent high tides from flooding London. Between the series of plates are a number of futuristic shapes, with massive concrete bases and clad above in metal, which house the machinery.

NATIONAL THEATRE

Built of bold, brutal concrete, many people find this building hideously ugly. Certainly when the concrete is wet, and the sky overcast, it does look gloomy and raw. However, the use of concrete creates opportunities which other materials could not achieve. The theatre occupies a fabulous position on the bank of the River Thames, with views upstream to Big Ben and the Palace of Westminster, and downstream to St Paul's Cathedral. The terraces and full-height glazing exploit this aspect to the full.

The internal foyers are dynamic and varied spaces, encouraging movement, informality and ad hoc performances by solo artists. The lush carpet contrasts with the rough texture of the concrete in a restrained interior.

I find the scale and proportions of the building attractive, but this, admittedly, is a minority view. It seems most people simply see crude concrete, and do not like it.

Copper

Lead and copper are extremely useful and versatile building materials. Lead is less dramatic in appearance but more widely used. Pliable but watertight, it is ideal for roofs, gutters, flashings, lanterns, hoppers, downpipes and so on.

Copper is light in weight and more unusual in colour. It is therefore more appropriate for complete and isolated roofs, rather than small bits of flashings and gutters.

AUDLEY END

Approached on the main road from Cambridge, this building suddenly explodes into sight. The bright green copper roof contrasts well with the Ketton stone walls, the river and lawns in the foreground, and the darker green backdrop of trees. A simple and very positive composition.

The grounds are the work of Lancelot 'Capability' Brown, who widened the river, introduced a 'ha-ha' and strategically placed clumps of trees in his matchless manner.

Fabric structures are being used more and more widely. They ought to be termed masted and membrane structures, as the material has to be held up in some way by a frame. Rather than simply being propped from underneath, like a tent, the tendency is to hang the membrane from wires suspended from high posts. The forces in this spider's web of wires and posts become extremely complex to calculate, and the building of fabric structures is inextricably linked to computer technology and three-dimensional modelling.

Fabric

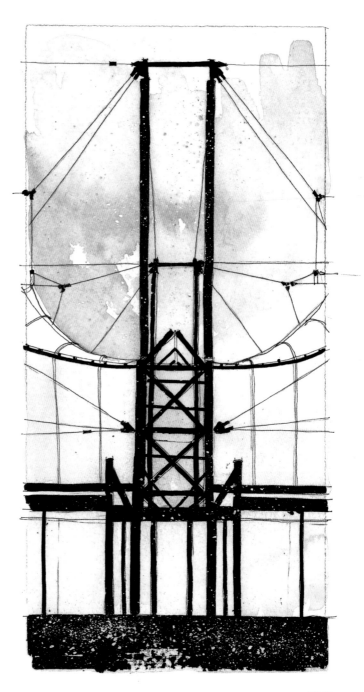

SCHLUMBERGER
Designed by Michael Hopkins and Partners, this building experiments with, and advances, the design of tensile fabric roofs. It creates a huge internal space used for experiments with drilling rigs; offices and laboratories are on either side.

The membrane roof is translucent and deceptively thin; the steel frame, its connectors and the thick tension wires give a clearer indication of the forces involved in supporting a roof as big as this.

The futuristic design sits very happily in the flat fen landscape to the West of Cambridge, and seems so much more appropriate to a pioneering building than the neo-vernacular nonsense built on many research parks. The Mound Stand at Lord's (see page 88) has an equally impressive fabric roof.

Colour

Most building materials are best left in their natural state. There are exceptions to this, particularly cement render, cob and pebbledash, where it has long been recognized that these look better with an applied colour. Historically, this would have been a mixture of lime and water, with a hint of powder colour. Today, the production of paint has become a sophisticated industry, and there is a multitude of different colours, compositions and textures from which to choose.

In terms of colour it is difficult to go too far wrong when using natural materials. Applied colour is another matter; in the right hands it can look entirely in keeping, adding emphasis or contrast. But all too easily applied colour can become lurid or discordant.

The choice of colour is very subjective and personal, and often runs in fashions. For example, the bright primary-coloured window frames, so popular in the early 1980s, now look crude and dated.

ABERAERON

Aberaeron is made up of groups and terraces of Georgian buildings of pleasant proportions. Once a busy port it now relies for its trade on the many holidaymakers, who are attracted by the unspoilt town, its remoteness from the motorway network (and hence fewer daytrippers), and the superb local scenery.

Colour plays a vital role in the appeal of Aberaeron, giving the elegant buildings a touch of spontaneity and individuality.

BRADNINCH

The buildings are ordinary but well maintained. Many are painted cob of which the decoration is kept in good order. It is the ordinariness of places like Bradninch that makes the point that colour has a vital role to play everywhere, in giving a sense of scale, recognition of the individual, and spontaneity.

SAFFRON WALDEN

Saffron Walden was a very wealthy town in the Middle Ages, benefiting from the wool trade and from the saffron crocus, which was used for medical purposes and as a dye. Its 16th- and 17th-century buildings are very fine with great richness of decorative plaster and ornate timberwork.

The plastered buildings were limewashed, which had to be done frequently as it quickly deteriorates in heavy rain. The buildings therefore accumulated so many layers that they formed a distinct layer of nearly one centimetre deep.

In Saffron Walden, and going eastwards into Suffolk, there seem to have been a particular fondness for pink, and quite delightful it is too.

TOBERMORY

The buildings of Tobermory surround a magnificent enclosed harbour. Individually they are of little consequence, but are brought to life by the richness of their colouring, and somehow the brightness of the colours works.

Although the surrounding countryside is almost sombre, and bright colour might seem too crude, the deep blues and reds, and the subtle yellows and pinks, give a sense of gaiety and liveliness entirely appropriate for a harbourside.

132☐

NORWICH: ELM STREET

Elm Street in Norwich consists mainly of Tudor and Georgian buildings. During the last century its condition deteriorated and it could easily have been swept away for a modern development.

Fortunately its qualities were recognized in time, and now Magdalen Street offers an example of what can be achieved by painstaking research. Instigated by the Civic Trust, colour experts developed a palette based on the colours and pigments available in the 18th and 19th centuries.

Stone Carving

Taken to its ultimate expression, stone carving is often the creation of an enormous picture telling a story; the West front of Wells Cathedral is the finest example. At the other extreme, the simplest of functional elements – a water spout, a gatepost or a door surround – could be enlivened by receiving extra care and time by a stone mason seeking an opportunity for artistic embellishment.

OXFORD: NEW COLLEGE

New College has a vast display of gargoyles – water spouts from concealed gutters which have been carved into grotesque bodies or heads.

Usually the rainwater discharges from the mouth of the unsightly figure.

MONTACUTE HOUSE: PAVILIONS

I have been to Montacute twice and each time one feature has remained in my memory. On the East side of the house is an immaculate lawn, like a huge billiard table. This is surrounded by a wall with balustrading and topped by obelisks. In the corners furthest from the house are two square pavilions, with semi-circular bay windows and ogee-shaped stone roofs with corner finials. Although dwarfed by the main house, their location and curvaceous form make these pavilions attractive elements within the overall composition of the estate.

ELY CATHEDRAL: PRIOR'S
DOOR
This late Norman doorway leads
from the South aisle of the
cathedral on to the cloisters. On
the far side were the Prior's
lodgings, and hence the name
for this door. The beautifully
carved stone framing the door is
in remarkable condition for its
age. The ornate iron door
brackets form an equally important part of the composition.

Advertising

The best forms of advertising (from a purely architectural standpoint) are those which relate directly to their surroundings – for example, a Victorian warehouse which has its name and the nature of its wares painted on its brick elevations. Advertising and buildings are then inextricably linked.

The worst advertising occurs when an enormous billboard obliterates the architecture behind, and the scale of its images overpower the surroundings.

PICCADILLY CIRCUS

This is an overrated space; much frequented by tourists, it carries constant traffic. The pavement on the South side bulges out to take in the Eros statue. The advertisements now seem lame in comparison with more innovative advertising thrown at us from other forms of media.

MICHELIN BUILDING

The Michelin Building was built in an art deco style on London's Fulham road in 1910, and is an excellent example of advertising being neatly absorbed into the fabric of the building itself. It is similar to the Oxo Building on the South Bank, where to overcome planning objections to advertising signs, high-level windows were shaped to spell 'Oxo'. At the Michelin Building, a huge window on the West side incorporates the Michelin Man himself.

□137

Lettering

This book began by looking at broad issues to do with the origin of towns, their settings and surroundings, and the large spaces within them. From considering the broad and the general it now ends with the narrow and the specific: quirky, one-off elements. The range is virtually limitless and the purpose of mentioning them is to remind us that no matter how hard we try to classify and generalize, most of our environment is composed of unique elements. Where they are particularly old, curious or well designed, we notice and remember them.

LLANGLOFFAN CHAPEL
Nonconformist chapels, mostly built in the 19th century, are notable and frequent contributors to the Welsh landscape. Their proportions are unusual in that they are squat, short buildings of simple and bold forms.

The Baptist church dated 1862 in Llangloffan, Pembrokeshire, is a typical example. The building is bold and the lettering looks remarkably modern.

Interesting Pieces

CHELTENHAM: POST BOX

Post boxes were introduced to this country in the middle of the 19th century; before then one had to take letters to central collection points.

All sorts of collection boxes have been designed. The residents of Bayshill Road in Cheltenham have this particularly attractive post box.

CHESTERFIELD SPIRE
Of all Britain's medieval wooden
church spires, the highest at 228
feet is on the Church of St
Mary's and All Saints at
Chesterfield. Presumed to be
twisted because of the use of
unseasoned timber, it is now
almost ten feet out of alignment,
and is the most well-known
feature of Chesterfield.

MACHYNLLETH: CLOCKTOWER

Machynlleth is a mid Wales market town which serves quite a large surrounding area. At the end of its main street there is a clocktower.

Built in 1872, the tower was commissioned by the Marquess of Londonderry, a local landowner, to celebrate the coming of age of his son and heir, and it is suitably exuberant and indulgent in style.

Final thoughts

I WROTE THIS BOOK because I enjoy visiting places, painting and writing. As the book has taken shape, I have become increasingly aware of another reason, which is that is I care about our environment. We have inherited a rich architectural heritage, which we have a responsibility to look after and, if possible, to enhance.

Inevitably, I have shown a highly selective and tiny representation of our inheritance. However, in studying this small selection, and by trying to analyse its essential characteristics, I have come to understand these places and buildings a little better.

This understanding of what we now possess is essential. In the past, because buildings were made of natural materials, usually local, they tended to blend with their surroundings, particularly over time. But today cheap and unattractive materials are readily available all over the country. The better man-made modern materials can fit in successfully, but only in the hands of skilful designers, of whom we have too few.

Over the past decade or so there has been a long debate about style, which has diverted attention from more important issues. There is a place for hi-tech; there is a place for historical revival. Whatever the style, what matters is the quality of its execution, and the response to the specific local context.

All too often these are lacking. In part this is because we simply do not comprehend our surroundings and our heritage, and so we cannot begin to know how we should relate to them with our contemporary contributions.

This book has modest aims. If you have enjoyed reading it, and celebrated with me all the wonderful places I have tried to describe with words and paint, I shall be pleased. If you have started to think, as I have more and more as the book has evolved, about how we should respond to our surroundings and shape them for future generations, then that will exceed my greatest expectations.

Roger FitzGerald
1995

YORK: THE SHAMBLES

Bibliography

I have referred to countless local leaflets, pamphlets and small guidebooks specific to particular towns and buildings. The following books have been of more general use and provide a comprehensive reading list.

Brunskill, Ron *Illustrated Handbook of Vernacular Architecture*, Faber and Faber, 1978

Clifton-Taylor, Alec *The Pattern of English Building*, Faber and Faber, 1987

————————. *Buildings of Delight*, Gollancz, 1988

Evans, Tony, and Candida Lycett-Green, *English Cottages*, Weidenfeld and Nicolson, 1982

Fletcher, Bannister *A History of Architecture*, Batsford, 1938

Gentleman, David *David Gentleman's Britain*, Weidenfeld and Nicolson, 1982

Girouard, Marc *The English Town*, Pothecary, 1990

Gore, Ann, and Laurence Fleming *Old English Villages*, Weidenfeld and Nicolson, 1986

Ingrams, Richard and John Piper *Piper's Places,* Chatto and Windus, 1983

Lloyd, David W. *The Making of English Towns*, Gollancz, 1984

Lowe, Jeremy Welsh *Industrial Workers' Housing 1775-1875,* National Museum of Wales, 1989

Morgan, Pete *The Yorkshire Ridings*, Gordon Fraser, 1987

Quiney, Anthony *The English Country Town,* Thames and Hudson, 1987

Wright, Christopher John *A Guide to the Pembrokeshire Coast Path,* Constable, 1986

Index